Until Peonies Bloom

The Complete Poems of
Kim Yeong-nang

Until Peonies Bloom

The Complete Poems of Kim Yeong-nang

Translated by Brother Anthony of Taizé

Introduction by Kim Seon-tae

A thing of beauty is a joy for ever.
—Keats

MERWIN
ASIA

Korean text Copyright © 2010 by Harold Kim Hyeon-cheol
Translation Copyright © 2010 by Brother Anthony of Taizé

All rights reserved. No part of this book may be reproduced in
any form without written permission from the publisher,
MerwinAsia, 59 West St., Unit 3W, Portland, ME 04102

MerwinAsia books are distributed by
St. Johann Press, P.O. Box 241, Haworth, NJ 07641

The translation and publication of this book were made possible
by the generosity of the Korean Literature Translation Institute

Library of Congress Cataloging-in-Publication Data

Kim, Yun-sik, 1903-1950.

[Poems. English & Korean]

Until peonies bloom : the complete poems of Kim Yeong-nang / foreword by Kim Seon-Tae ;
translated by Brother Anthony of Taizé. — Bilingual ed.

p. cm.

ISBN 978-1-878282-98-9 (pbk. : alk. paper)

1. Kim, Yun-sik, 1903-1950--Translations into English.

I. Anthony, of Taizé, Brother, 1942- II. Title.

PL991.415.Y8A2 2010

895.7'13—dc22

2009052639

First printing in hardcover, April 2010
ISBN 978-1-878282-83-5

Printed in the United States of America

The paper used in this publication meets the minimum requirements of the
American National Standard for Information Services—Permanence of Paper for
Printed Library Materials, ANSI/NISO Z39/48-1992

Contents

Introduction: Professor Kim Seon-tae — vii

Translator's Note — xv

Poems 1930–1935 — 1

Quatrains — 57

Poems 1938–1940 — 73

Poems 1946–1950 — 107

Memories of My Father: Harold Kim Hyeon-cheol — 151

Poem Titles — 163

About the Translator — 167

Introduction

Professor Kim Seon-tae
Korean Department, Mokpo University

The Poet's Life

The poet known today as Kim Yeong-nang (1903–1950) was originally given the name Kim Yun-sik, Yeong-nang being the pen name under which he published his work. He was born in Gangjin, South Jeolla Province. His father, Kim Jong-ho, was a wealthy landowner; the poet was the first-born of five sons and two daughters. In 1911, after studying for two years in a traditional Confucian school, young Kim Yun-sik entered Gangjin Primary School, graduating in 1915. In 1916, following the old Korean tradition of the region, he was married to Kim Eun-cho, who, two years his senior, died the following year. In February 1916, he went up to Seoul where he studied English at the Central Christian School before enrolling in March 1917 in Huimun-uisuk School (now known as Huimun High School). He was in his third year there when the Independence Movement began with nationwide demonstrations on March 1, 1919. Kim was arrested, along with many others, and spent some time in detention. Once released, he returned to his home in Gangjin, where he continued to be active in the Independence Movement and was again arrested. He was held in Daegu Prison for three months before being transferred to the police detention cells in Gangjin and Jangheung for another three months.

He gave up his studies at Huimun-uisuk School in the autumn of 1919. Crossing to Japan in September 1920, he completed secondary studies at Aoyama Gakuin in Tokyo. It was here that he first met Bak Yong-cheol (1904-1938), the poet and critic, who was a close source of support in later years. In the summer of 1921, Kim visited Gangjin and told his parents of his wish to study singing. Because his father was strongly opposed to this, he ended up enrolling in the English Department of Aoyama Gakuin, where he studied Western literature, becoming enthralled with such romantic poets as W.B. Yeats, Paul Verlaine, Keats and Shelley. He met radical Koreans in Japan, including the renowned anarchist Bak Yeol. On September 1, 1923, the terrible Kanto earthquake devasted Tokyo, and in November Kim returned to his native land. In the course of 1924 he developed a relationship with Choi Seung-hui, a great beauty who later became a celebrated dancer, but both families were opposed to their engagement, and in 1925 he married An Gui-ryeon (1906-1989), a teacher at Lucia Girls' High School in Wonsan.

Early in 1930, Kim Yeong-nang was part of a group that included the poets Jeong Ji-yong, Byeon Yeong-ro, and Yi Ha-yun who, together with Bak Yong-cheol, decided that there was a need for a regular poetry review in which they could publish their work. On March 5, the review *Simunhak* (Poetry) was launched by the Simunhak Company, and the group became known as the Simunhak-pa. Kim began his career as a recognized poet with the publication in the review of the poem "*Dongbaekipei pitnanun maum*" (A heart reflected in camellia petals). In 1935, he combined the thirty-six poems he had published in the review and in *Munhak* (Literature) with seventeen unpublished poems to produce his first collection, *Yeongnang Sichip* (Yeongnang's poems). There were three periods in his life when Kim Yeong-nang wrote nothing. The first was from November 1931 until December 1933, the second from December 1935 until August 1938. The third, by far the longest, extended from September 1940 until November 1946. So during eleven of the twenty years after he began to publish, he wrote nothing.

The third period of silence, in particular, must be seen as a form of protest and resistance to the increasingly repressive, militaristic Japanese occupation of Korea. Kim Yeong-nang is celebrated in Korea for his refusal, almost unparalleled among writers, to submit to the demands of the Japanese authorities. All citizens were under intense pressure to offer regular worship at the Japanese Shintō shrines, and many who refused were imprisoned, even killed.

Until the very end, Kim Yeong-nang never entered a shrine. During the war, especially, Koreans were told they must change their Korean names into Japanese ones as a sign of patriotism. Kim Yeong-nang not only refused for himself but would not allow his children to change their names, although the schools they were attending threatened to expel them if they did not. The Japanese obliged all male Koreans to have their hair cut very short, in convict style, but until the end of the war on August 15, 1945, Kim Yeong-nang wore his hair long. His resistance was equally clearly expressed in the traditional Korean clothes he proudly wore whenever he went out. He loved traditional Korean music, playing it himself, and often invited singers of *pansori* to perform in his house.

Although certain poets resisted Japan so actively that they were imprisoned and killed, extremely few writers were able to resist to such a degree as Kim, in part because of their need to earn a living. Kim Yeong-nang survived by gradually selling his family's land. His pride in Korea's poetic and cultural traditions was surely inspired by a strong awareness of belonging to an aristocratic family. The actively pro-Japanese attitudes of many writers and intellectuals stand in stark contrast to his quiet but firm refusal to submit; in later years some of these writers even tried to belittle his resistance in order to disguise their own shameful record. He went so far as to challenge Japanese authority by writing an essay praising two great Koreans of the past, the poet Yun Seon-do and the great thinker Dasan Jeong Yak-yong in 1938, by which time the official Japanese position was that Korea had no cultural achievements worth celebrating. Kim Yeong-nang was a courageous writer who refused to deny or denigrate his nation's past.

As soon as Korea was liberated from Japan at the end of the war, new dangers and divisions appeared. Right- and left-wing sympathizers grew increasingly far apart, reflecting the division between the North under Soviet supervision and the South under the Americans. In addition to being the head of the then right-wing-leaning Korean Young Men's Association in Gangjin, Kim Yeong-nang was active in groups such as the Korean Independence Promotion Assembly, which was the origin of many social groups working for the new Korean government. As a result, he risked becoming the target of terrorist attacks emanating from the Communist

Party. He continued to live in Gangjin until May 1948, when he stood as a candidate for the first Constitutional Assembly but failed to be elected; he then moved to Seoul and received a government position in the department responsible for publishing. He resigned after eight months, however, being too independent-minded to be able to establish good relations with his superiors. He approached the well-placed younger poet Seo Jeong-ju for help in having his second collection of poems published, asking him to write the epilogue. As a result, *Yeongnang Siseon* (Yeongnang, selected poems) was published in October 1949.

When the North Koreans captured Seoul at the start of the Korean War in June 1950, Kim Yeong-nang and his family were unable to leave Seoul. During the months of Communist occupation he hid in the house of relatives, where his family later joined him. He thus avoided being kidnapped by the North Koreans. However, he died on September 29, 1950, after being hit by shrapnel during the bombardment of the city as the North Korean forces were withdrawing. He was only forty-seven. He left behind eighty-six poems and fifteen prose pieces. Later, the house where he and his family had lived in Gangjin was restored as a memorial, and visitors are often bewildered by the complete lack of personal relics there. The reason is that when his grieving family returned to the house in Seoul where they had been living until the start of the war, they found it completely ransacked and gutted. Not one of the poet's books, papers, or personal belongings had survived.

The Poetry

If we consider Kim Yeong-nang's poetry written between 1930 and 1935 as the "early poems," we might want to distinguish between poems tending to express a pessimistic world view and those evoking an ideal world. Poems expressing an affinity with nature or celebrating his home region can be considered to be idealizing, while the far more numerous melancholy poems represent what we might call a pessimistic direction. The two are united by the overriding pure lyricism common to all. The beautiful region around Gangjin has long been considered a pleasant area in which to live, and those poems which express a love of his home region are marked by a lyricism inspired by a close affinity with nature. The resilience of camellia leaves inspires a deep sense of wonder; the vigor of spring or the brightness of autumn awaken corresponding sentiments in the poet. Certain poems that depend strongly on the characteristics of the local dialect for their effect are indicative of an idealization of the poet's home region. However, it seems important to go beyond the notions of idealization or the individual association with home and to see here images symbolizing a commitment to the value of Korea itself as nation. The same national reference can then also be found in retrospect in the poems indicating melancholy or resistance.

When it comes to the poems indicating a darker pessimism, again we are alert to the feelings inspired by the situation of Korea under Japanese colonial rule. On a more personal note, there is also the sorrow caused by the sudden loss of his first wife. The pessimism is another source of the melancholy tone found in so many poems, where we find repeated use of word like "tears," "death," or "sorrow." The poem "At the Tip of the Gangseondae Rock Pinacle" is characteristic of this theme, being clearly something other than an evocation of an actual location; rather it turns much more toward despairing feelings of pointlessness and loss, if not indeed a desire for self-destruction in order to attain a transcendent world beyond this one.

The poems written between 1938 and 1940 constitute a second period in his writing. They are marked by stronger, more direct resistance to the Japanese occupation. The dominant themes expressed in many of these often very pessimistic poems are death and frustration. These were years when the Japanese military were exercising an increasingly harsh control over the country, while more and more Korean writers were expressing pro-Japanese sentiments. Perhaps as a result, Kim Yeong-nang turns from the preoccupation with his own inner world found in the early poems to a concern with the realities of the outside world.

In the poem "Geomungo" published in January 1938 we find the lines: "Outside are wild lands where packs of wolves roam, / groups of apes gambol, only seemingly human." It seems fairly clear that this is an allegory for the Japanese and their Korean henchmen, while the "kirin" referred to in the poem, which is the name of a mythical animal that defends threatened purity, is less a silent musical instrument than the poet's own heart, unable to find anything to sing joyfully about in such a situation. The poem "Carrying Poison," published in November that year, contains the strongest statement of resistance in its last line: "Bearing poison still, I will readily go, / to save my lonely soul on the last day of my life." Finally, in "Chunhyang," published in 1940, we find the supreme vision of national resistance. In the traditional story, the girl Chunhyang remains faithful to her absent love despite the threats and tortures of the wicked magistrate, convinced that the day will come when she will be vindicated and preferring death to surrender. The symbolic parallel with Korea's lost national identity is very clear, and Kim Yeong-nang seems to identify his own resistance with that of the courageous Chunhyang, though in a rather dramatically pessimistic manner.

When he started to write again in 1945, after the years of silence during the Pacific War, Korea had been liberated from Japan but was far from being at peace. In the years between 1945 and the outbreak of the Korean War on June 25, 1950, there was constant turmoil as radically different regimes arose in the South and the North. At the same time, the struggle for power in the South between "left" and "right" resulted in massacres, guerrilla warfare, and fierce ideological confrontations while Syngman Rhee, supported by the United States, was establishing the Republic of Korea. Kim Yeong-nang wrote poems in support of the emerging nation, but he could not ignore the tragedy of the ideological conflict. As a result, his later poems often waver between hope and despair. The first poem written in this new situation was "Drum," with its evocation of the lively, dynamic rhythms of traditional Korean drumming. Equally optimistic and future-oriented is the poem "Let's Go Down to the Sea," with its enthusiastic evocation of the newly liberated Korean people's freedom and potential as stars and jewels: "We are unfettered souls, a liberated people, / eagerly embracing a myriad stars." It is important to note that many Korean poets have chosen this as his finest poem, rather than the purely lyrical "Until Peonies Bloom," which has become his token poem through its inclusion in school textbooks. He was much more than simply a writer of disembodied lyric poems.

Himself forced to leave Gangjin after threats against his life and property, he soon found himself writing poems about the terrible fratricidal divisions between ideologies and parties that were tearing society apart. The community of writers was not spared, of course. The poems "Execution Yard at Dawn" and "Despair" give a clear indication of the poet's profound anguish at what was happening. He is far from defending one side against the other; his great concern is that these terrible things are being done by brother to brother, and it is young people, the hope of the nation, who are killing one another as guerrillas, soldiers, and militiamen. The result is the dark sorrow expressed in "Kite 2," in which the childhood loss of a kite previously evoked in his early poem "Kite 1" becomes a symbol of the hope he had nourished in 1945, but has now lost. The loss is no longer personal but national: "a flickering spark expires. / Ah! A life, and the country too, all fade far away." This feeling of despair turns into something approaching a death wish in the poem "Forgetfulness," one of his most anguished and pessimistic works: "for some reason nowadays I keep feeling that death is approaching." He is far from the romantic melancholy of certain early poems. This death is national, not personal, and indicates an almost prophetic awareness of the approaching outbreak of fratricidal war.

In Context

First, there can be no doubt as to the outstanding role of Kim Yeong-nang in the development of the pure lyric in twentieth-century Korean poetry. In recent years, scholars have stressed the significance of the group of poets to which he belonged at the start of his career, the "Simunhak-pa." He was undoubtedly the leading poet of that group. The native Korean tradition of pure lyricism which they espoused can be traced back to Kim Sowol in the 1920s and continues with the emergence of Seo Jeong-ju in the later 1930s. It has become customary in Korea to characterize the lyrical tone of their poetry as "feminine." They were especially attentive to poetic diction, seeking words with a particular sensual impact. For Kim Yeong-nang, influenced by Paul Verlaine's "De la musique avant toute chose" (music above all) ("Art poétique"), musicality was one of the fundamental characteristics of the lyric, and it is the musical quality of his poems that has made him particularly influential in the history of modern Korean poetry.

Second, he may also be considered a leading poet in that by refining poetic language, the poet brings a national language to its perfection. With his innate feeling for language, Kim Yeong-nang selected and arranged words in such a way as to exploit to the full their delicate resonance and nuances, while showing outstanding skill in the use of dialect and rhythm. The manner in which he used traditional rhythms to express feelings of sorrow and longing was particularly well-adapted to the lyrical expression of such a dark age. His delicate sensitivity in using words is the result of his skill in blending objects and experiences into a single aesthetic impression.

Third, while Korea lay fettered under Japanese colonial rule, Kim Yeong-nang remained ever faithful to his role as a poet of national resistance. In this, his record is unparalleled. In 1919, still a high-school student, he was imprisoned for his leading role in the Gangjin Independence Movement. When the Japanese oppression was at its height, he alone in Gangjin refused to change his name or offer worship at the Shinto shrine. In addition, ever steadfast, he has the honor of being one of the very rare Korean writers who never wrote a single pro-Japanese line. More than that, he risked his life by expressing constant, intense anti-Japanese sentiments in poems such as "Geomungo," "Full of Poison," etc. As a result, he deserves to be celebrated, not simply as a great lyricist, but as a poet of heroic national resistance unequalled during the whole period of Japanese oppression.

Translator's Note

The translations follow the order of the texts found in *Kim Yeong-nang jeonjip*, edited by Kim Hak-dong, Seoul 1993, Munhaksegyesa. This edition presents the poems in the chronological order of their composition / publication. However, the poems included in *Yeongnang Siseon* (Yeongnang, selected poems), published in October 1949, benefitted from the direct supervision of the poet, by then living in Seoul, and from the editorial suggestions made by the younger but already much-admired poet Midang Seo Jeong-ju. As a result, the poems already published in *Yeongnang Sichip* (Yeongnang's poems) in 1935 or elsewhere were sometimes revised, or at least given new titles. In the translations, the 1949 revisions have been accepted, and the variations from the original publication are noted at the end of each poem.

The poem "Geumho-gang" (Geumho River) is no longer attributed to Kim Yeong-nang and has been omitted. The poem "Lying in the Middle of the Road" was only recently included in the list of the poet's works, having been wrongly attributed to another poet. While translating, various generally recognized misprints in the Korean originals have been silently corrected. The translations of certain poems owe much to the as yet unpublished research of Professor Kim Seon-tae of the Korean Department, Mokpo University, to whom I am deeply grateful. I am even more grateful to him for having consented to write the above Introduction.

My chief debt of gratitude must be to Kim Hyeon-Cheol, the poet's son, who first asked me to undertake these translations, who has carefully read them, and who has suggested many corrections. I am equally grateful to Professor Lee Soong-Won of Seoul Women's University, who has just published a new edition of the original poems, and who has helped immensely in preparing the Korean text for this edition

Until Peonies Bloom

The Complete Poems of
Kim Yeong-nang

Poems 1930–1935

끝없는 강물이 흐르네

내 마음의 어딘 듯 한편에 끝없는 강물이 흐르네
돋쳐 오르는 아침 날빛이 빤질한 은결을 돋우네
가슴엔 듯 눈엔 듯 또 핏줄엔 듯
마음이 도른도른 숨어 있는 곳
내 마음의 어딘듯 한편에 끝없는 강물이 흐르네

1935 제목: 동백 잎에 빛나는 마음

An Endless River Flows

Somewhere in my heart, it seems, an endless river flows.
The dawn's rising glow brightens its smooth, silvery path.
In my breast, it seems, my eyes, my veins,
where my heart hides whispering,
somewhere in my heart, it seems, endlessly a river flows.

1935 title: "A Heart Reflected in a Camellia Leaf."

어덕에 바로 누워

어덕에 바로 누워
아슬한 푸른 하늘 뜻 없이 바래다가
나는 잊었습네 눈물 도는 노래를
그 하늘 아슬하여 너무도 아슬하여

이 몸이 서러운 줄 어덕이야 아시련만
마음의 가는 웃음 한때라도 없더라냐
아슬한 하늘 아래 귀여운 맘 즐거운 맘
내 눈은 감기었데 감기었데

As I Lay Stretched Out on a Hill

As I lay stretched out on a hill
staring absentmindedly at the blue sky far away,
I completely forgot tearful songs,
for that sky was so distant, too far away by far.

Though this hill might know my sorrows,
can there never be even a slight smile in my heart?
Beneath the far-away sky, a lovely heart, a merry heart,
and my eyes have closed, have closed.

"오-매 단풍 들겄네"

"오-매 단풍 들겄네"
장광에 골불은 감잎 날러오아
누이는 놀란 듯이 치어다보며
"오-매 단풍 들겄네"

추석이 내일모레 기둘리리
바람이 잦이어서 걱정이리
누이의 마음아 나를 보아라
"오-매 단풍 들겄네"

1935 제목: 누이의 마음아 나를 보아라

"Why, Autumn Colors Are Coming!"

"Why, autumn colors are coming!"
Red persimmon leaves fly above the crocks in the yard;
my sister gazes up in seeming surprise:
"Why, autumn colors are coming!"

In a couple of days it will be the day for autumn ancestral rites;
wind often blows, I am worried;
heart of my sister, look at me.
"Why, autumn colors are coming!"

1935 title: "Heart of My Sister, Look at Me."

제야(除夜)

제운 밤 촛불이 찌르르 녹아 버린다
못 견디게 무거운 어느 별이 떨어지는가

어둑한 골목골목에 수심은 떴다 갈앉었다
제운 맘 이 한밤이 모질기도 하온가

희부얀 종이 등불 수줍은 걸음걸이
샘물 정히 떠 붓는 안쓰러운 마음결

한 해라 그리운 정을 몽고 쌓아 흰 그릇에
그대는 이 밤이라 맑으라 비사이다

New Year's Eve

On the last night of the year the candles melt away.
Are any stars falling, too heavy to endure?

Down every twilit valley, melancholy is rising, falling.
Is this New Year's Eve so harsh?

With a dim paper lantern, a bashful demeanor,
painstakingly you draw up fresh water, pour it out.

Over the white bowl heaped with a whole year's love,
you pray that this night be bright.

Note: This poem evokes the traditional way women used to pray over a bowl of freshly drawn water.

쓸쓸한 뫼 앞에

쓸쓸한 뫼 앞에 후젓이 앉으면
마음은 갈앉은 양금 줄같이
무덤의 잔디에 얼굴을 부비면
넋이는 향 맑은 구슬손같이
산골로 가노라 산골로 가노라
무덤이 그리워 산골로 가노라

Before a Desolate Grave

If I sit alone at the foot of a desolate grave

my heart is like the silent strings of a zither.

If I rub my face on the grass of the grave

my soul, like an incense-fragrant jeweled hand,

makes for the hills, makes for the hills;

yearning for a grave, it makes for the hills.

함박눈

바람이 부는 대로 찾아가오리
홀린 듯 기약하신 님이시기로
행여나! 행여나! 귀를 종금이
어리석다 하심은 너무로구려

문풍지 설움에 몸이 저리어
내리는 함박눈 가슴 해어져
헛보람! 헛보람! 몰랐으로만
날더러 어리석단 너무로구려

1935 제목: 원망

Falling Snowflakes

"I will come visiting as the wind blows."
Dearest one, you made promises as if possessed.
Maybe! Maybe! I long to hear that voice.
Calling me a fool for that would be too harsh.

My body's numbed by sorrow, wind whistles through chinks in the door,
my breast is worn threadbare by falling snowflakes;
I never realized it was futile to seek a recompense, quite futile,
but telling me I'm a fool for that would be too harsh

1935 title: "Reproach."

돌담에 속삭이는 햇발

돌담에 속삭이는 햇발같이
풀 아래 웃음 짓는 샘물같이
내 마음 고요히 고운 봄 길 위에
오늘 하루 하늘을 우러르고 싶다

새악시 볼에 떠오는 부끄럼같이
시의 가슴을 살프시 젖는 물결같이
보드레한 에메랄드 얇게 흐르는
실비단 하늘을 바라보고 싶다

1935 제목: 내 마음 고요히 고은 봄 길 위에

Sunlight Whispering on Stone Walls

Like sunlight whispering on stone walls,
like spring-water smiling under grass,
today, on a lovely spring road my heart longs
to gaze quietly up at the sky, all day long.

Like shyness infusing a young woman's cheeks,
like ripples gently caressing a poem's breast,
I long to gaze up at the silken sky
as it flows thin, a soft emerald hue.

1935 title: "Quietly on a Lonely Spring Road, My Heart."

꿈 밭에 봄마음

굽어진 돌담을 돌아서 돌아서
달이 흐른다 놀이 흐른다
하이얀 그림자
은실을 즈르르 말아서
꿈 밭에 봄마음 가고 가고 또 간다

A Springtime Heart Off to Fields in Dreams

Turning, turning round crooked stone walls,

the moon flows on, twilight flows on,

white shadows

pursue a trickle of silver threads,

a springtime heart sets off, sets off, off to fields in dreams.

가늘한 내음

내 가슴속에 가늘한 내음
애끈히 떠도는 내음
저녁 해 고요히 지는 제
먼 산 허리에 슬리는 보랏빛

오! 그 수심뜬 보랏빛
내가 잃은 마음의 그림자
한 이틀 정열에 뚝뚝 떨어진 모란의
깃든 향취가 이 가슴 놓고 갔을 줄이야

얼결에 여읜 봄 흐르는 마음
헛되이 찾으려 허덕이는 날
뻘 위에 철썩 갯물이 놓이듯
얼컥 이는 훗근한 내음

아! 훗근한 내음 내키다마는
서어한 가슴에 그늘이 도나니
수심뜨고 애끈하고 고요하기
산 허리에 슬리는 저녁 보랏빛

Faint Perfume

The faint perfume in my heart,
the perfume drifting anxiously,
the purple glow hanging over distant mountains
as the evening sun quietly sets,

Ah, that purple glow so full of sorrow,
the shadow of the heart I've lost,
the deep fragance of peonies that drop, drop after two days of passion
was bound to go, leaving this heart behind.

One day as I was gasping, seeking in vain
spring's flowing heart I had lost in a flash,
a hot perfume came rising
like the tide spreading over mudflats.

Ah, the hot perfume spreads
but a shadow has fallen on my wavering heart,
so sorrowful, anxious, still,
an eventide purple glow that fades on mountainsides . . .

내 옛날 온 꿈이

내 옛날 온 꿈이 모조리 실리어 간
하늘가 닿는 데 기쁨이 사신가

고요히 사라지는 구름을 바래자
헛되나 마음 가는 그곳뿐이라

눈물을 삼키며 기쁨을 찾노란다
허공은 저리도 한없이 푸르름을

엎디어 눈물로 땅 위에 새기자
하늘가 닿는 데 기쁨이 사신다

1935 제목: 하늘가 닿는 데

Dreams I Used to Have

Does joy dwell where the sky meets the earth,
where every dream I ever dreamed has been taken?

As I bid farewell to each quietly vanishing cloud
I know it's pointless but that is the place my heart tends toward.

Swallowing tears, I seek for joy.
Then the heavens above are so infinitely blue.

I long to fall prostrate and write on the ground with my tears:
"Joy dwells where the sky meets the earth."

1935 title: "Where the Sky Meets the Earth."

내 마음을 아실 이

내 마음을 아실 이
내 혼자 마음 날같이 아실 이
그래도 어데나 계실 것이면

내 마음에 때때로 어리우는 티끌과
속임 없는 눈물의 간곡한 방울방울
푸른 밤 고이 맺는 이슬 같은 보람을
보낸 듯 감추었다 내어 드리지

아! 그립다
내 혼자 마음 날같이 아실 이
꿈에나 아득히 보이는가

향 맑은 옥돌에 불이 달아
사랑은 타기도 하오련만
불빛에 연긴 듯 희미론 마음은
사랑도 모르리 내 혼자 마음은

Someone Who Knows My Heart

If somewhere someone exists
who knows my heart,
who knows my solitary heart as I do,

the dust that sometimes clouds my heart,
and the pleading drops of guileless tears,
the rewards that gently form like dew in azure nights:
all these I would lay like hidden treasures before that person.

Ah, such yearning.
Can I see far off in my dreams
one who knows my solitary heart as I do?

In pure-scented jade, flames glow red;
I wish that love would kindle too,
but my heart, clouded like a smoking lamp,
knows no love, my solitary heart.

시냇물 소리

바람 따라 가지 오고 멀어지는 물소리
아주 바람같이 쉬는 적도 있었으면
흐름도 가득 찰랑 흐르다가
더러는 그림같이 머물렀다 흘러 보지
밤도 산골 쓸쓸하이 이 한밤 쉬어 가지
어느 뉘 꿈에 든 셈 소리 없든 못할소냐

새벽 잠결에 언뜻 들리어
내 무건 머리 선뜻 씻기우느니
황금 소반에 구슬이 굴렀다
오 그립고 향미론 소리야
물아 거기 좀 멈췄으라 나는 그윽이
저 창공의 은하 만년을 헤아려 보노니

The Sound of a Stream

Borne on the wind, the sound of a stream comes close then fades.

If only it would stop and linger, like the wind.

I wish the stream would flow, so I can feel it brimming full,

then stay a while like a painting, before flowing on again.

The night lingers, pitying the valley's solitude; the stream might stay here

as if stealing into someone's dream—even if there it is soundless.

Abruptly I hear it at dawn as I sleep,

washing round my heavy head

like jewels rolling on a golden tray!

Oh, sound I so long for, so full of fragrance, stay!

While you linger here, I long to ponder in my heart

the eternity of the Milky Way above.

뉘 눈결에 쏘이었소

뉘 눈결에 쏘이었소
온통 수줍어진 저 하늘빛
담 안에 복숭아꽃이 붉고
밖에 봄은 벌써 재앙스럽소

꾀꼬리 단둘이 단둘이로다
빈 골짝도 부끄러워
혼란스런 노래로 흰 구름 피어올리나
그 속에 든 꿈이 더 재앙스럽소

Stung by a Look

Stung by someone's look,
the sky is blushing bashfully;
the peach flowers inside the wall glow red,
while spring is mischievous outside.

Orioles go in twos, in twos,
even empty valleys blush,
at their confused songs white clouds rise high,
the dreams they contain are more mischievous still.

눈물에 실려 가면

눈물에 실려 가면 산길로 칠십 리
돌아보니 찬바람 무덤에 몰리네
서울이 천 리로다 멀기도 하련만
눈물에 실려 가면 한 걸음 한 걸음

뱃장 위에 부은 발 쉬일까 보다
달빛으로 눈물을 말릴까 보다
고요한 바다 위로 노래가 떠간다
설움도 부끄러워 노래가 노래가

Borne on Tears

Borne on tears, seventy *ri* along mountain paths,
I look back; cold winds are striking the graves.
Seoul is a thousand *ri* away, that's far but
once borne on tears, a single step, a single step . . .

I long to rest my swollen feet on the floor of a boat,
to have moonlight dry my tears.
Songs go floating away over a quiet sea.
Ashamed of sorrow, singing, singing . . .

Note. seventy *ri*: 10 *ri* = 4 kilometers, 70 *ri* = 28 kilometers, 1,000 *ri* = 400 kilometers.

그대는 호령도 하실 만하다

창랑에 잠방거리는 흰 물새러냐
그대는 탈도 없이 태연스럽다

마을 휩쓸고 목숨 앗아간
간밤 풍랑도 가소롭구나

아침 날빛에 돛 높이 달고
청산아 보아라 떠나가는 배

바람은 차고 물결은 치고
그대는 호령도 하실 만하다

1935 첫연 첫행; 창랑에 잠방거리는 섬들을 길러

You Are Worthy to Speak in a Commanding Tone

Are those white birds lapped by blue waves?
You remain calm and all is well.

Last night's sea storm that overwhelmed the village,
taking lives, to you is laughable.

"Behold me, you green hills," that ship
is setting forth, sails raised high in the morning light.

The wind may be cold, the waves swell high,
you are worthy to speak in a commanding tone.

Line 1, 1935: "You raised isles lapped by blue waves."

아파 누워

아파 누워 혼자 비노라
이대로 가진 못하느냐

비는 마음 그래도 거짓 있나
사잔 욕심 찾아도 보나
새삼스레 있을 리 없다
힘없고 느릿한 핏줄 하나

오! 그저 이슬같이
예사 고요히 지려무나
저기 은행잎은 떠 날은다

Lying Sick Alone, I Pray

Lying sick alone, I pray:
Please, let me depart like this.

I try to see if my praying heart is lying,
if I long to go on living;
surely, there is no cause for that?
One feeble, sluggish trickle of blood.

Oh! I shall depart very quietly
just like the dew.
Out there, gingko leaves are flying.

물 보면 흐르고

물 보면 흐르고
별 보면 또렷한
마음이 어이면 늙으뇨

흰날에 한숨만
끝없이 떠돌던
시절이 가엾고 멀어라

안쓰런 눈물에 안겨
흩은 잎 쌓인 곳에 빗방울 드듯
느낌은 후줄근히 흘러흘러 가건만

그 밤을 흘히 앉으면
무심코 야윈 볼도 만져 보느니
시들고 못 피인 꽃 어서 떨어지거라

At the Sight of Water

At the sight of water, my heart flows;
at the sight of stars, my heart is clear.
How then can my heart grow old?

How pitiful and far away,
the days when I ceaselessly roamed,
uttering sighs on bright clear days.

Embraced in a regretful tear,
as a raindrop falls where scattered leaves pile high,
feelings limply, simply flow.

If I sit all alone on such a night
and lightly caress a haggard cheek,
withering, unblooming flowers quickly fall.

강선대(降仙臺) 돌바늘 끝에

강선대 돌바늘 끝에
하잔한 인간 하나
그는 벌써
불타오르는 호수에 뛰어내려서
제 몸 살랐더라면 좋았을 인간

이제 몇 해뇨
그 황홀 맛나도 이 몸 선뜻 못 내던지고
그 찬란 보고도 노래는 영영 못 부른 채
젖어드는 물결과 싸우다 넘기고
시달린 마음이라 더러 눈물 맺었네

강선대 돌바늘 끝에 벌써
불살랐어야 좋았을 인간

At the Tip of the Gangseondae Rock Pinacle

At the tip of the Gangseondae rock pinacle
stands someone insignificant,
someone who would have done far better
to have thrown himself down by now
into a burning lake.

How many years has it been?
Even if I encountered such ecstasy, I could never simply throw down this body.
Even if I saw such splendor, I could never sing.
Passing beyond after fighting soaking waves,
my heart felt so troubled that tears kept welling up.

Someone stands at the tip of the Gangseondae rock pinacle
who would have done far better to have thrown himself down by now.

Note: There are a number of beautiful rock formations with this name, which suggests that immortals once descended to enjoy their beauty. The poet may have been evoking the most celebrated one, in Myohyang-san, in what is now North Korea.

사개 틀린 고풍(古風)의 툇마루에

사개 틀린 고풍의 툇마루에 없는 듯이 앉아
아직 떠오를 기척도 없는 달을 기다린다
아무런 생각 없이
아무런 뜻 없이

이제 저 감나무 그림자가
사뿐 한치씩 옮아오고
이 마루 위에 빛깔의 방석이
보시시 깔리우면

나는 내 하나인 외론 벗
가냘폰 내 그림자와
말 없이 몸짓 없이 서로 맞대고 있으려니
이 밤 옮기는 발짓이나 들려오리라

On an Old-style Twisted Dovetail Back-porch

I sit quietly on an old-style twisted dovetail back-porch
and wait for the moon that as yet gives no sign of rising,
without one thought,
without one wish.

Soon that persimmon tree's shadow
will move closer, inch by inch,
once a colored cushion has been laid
on the porch's floor.

Then I and my one lonely companion,
my slender shadow,
will find ourselves face to face without a word or a gesture.
I might even hear night's approaching footsteps.

불지암(佛地庵)

그 밤 가득한 산 정기는 기척 없이 솟은 하얀 달빛에 모두 쓸리우고
한낮을 향미로우라 울리던 시냇물 소리마저 멀고 그윽하여
중향(衆香)의 맑은 돌에 맺은 금 이슬 구을러 흐트듯
아담한 꿈 하나 여승의 호젓한 품을 애끈히 사라졌느니

천년 옛날 쫓기어 간 신라의 아들이냐 그 빛은 청초한 수미산 나리꽃
정녕 지름길 섯들은 흰옷 입은 고운 소년이
흡사 그 바다에서 이 바다로 고요히 떨어지는 별살같이
옆 산모롱이에 언뜻 나타나 앞 골 시내로 사뿐 사라지심

승은 아까워 못 견디는 양 희미해지는 꿈만 뒤쫓았으나
끝없는지라 돌여 밝는 날의 남모를 귀한 보람을 품었을 뿐
토끼라 사슴만 뛰어 보여도 반듯이 그려지는 사나이 지났었느니

고운 연(輦)의 거동이 있음 직한 맑고 트인 날 해는 기우는 제
승의 보람은 이루었느냐 가엾어라 미목 청수한 젊은 선비
앞 시냇물 모이는 새파란 소에 몸을 던지시니라

(불지암은 내금강 유적한 곳에 허물어져 가는 고찰 두 젊은 승이 그의 스님을 뫼시고 있다)

1935 제목 : 불지암 서정

Bulji-am, Buddha-World Hermitage

The mountain spirits that filled the night were all swept away by a burst of white moonlight,
the sound of the stream that echoed, making the daytime fair, withdrew and grew faint.
Just as golden dew pearls and flows over the bright stones of the Strong Fragrance,
one dainty dream vanished in anguish from a nun's lonely heart.

Was it a prince of old Silla sent into exile a thousand years ago?
His complexion was that of a graceful lily on Mount Sumeru.
For sure a cute lad in white clothes taking a short cut in a hurry, like starlight falling quietly from one sea to another,
abruptly appearing round a mountain spur then vanishing softly following the stream down the valley ahead.

Filled with a regret she could not endure, the nun set off in pursuit of her fading dream
but it proved endless and all she preserved was a glimpse in broad daylight, a precious sign.
Even a rabbit or a deer seen speeding by reminded her of the man she so cherished, who had gone away.

Was the nun's wish fulfilled at sunset one clear, cloudless day
when a royal sedan might well be on the move?
Alas, that good-looking young scholar threw himself into the azure pond where the water of the stream gathered.

(Poet's Note: Bulji hermitage is a decaying temple in a secluded part of the Inner Diamond Mountains. There two young monks are caring for their master.)

1935 title: "Bulji-am Lyric."

Note: The "Strong Fragrance" Falls are better known as "Nine Dragon Falls."

모란이 피기까지는

모란이 피기까지는
나는 아직 나의 봄을 기다리고 있을 테요
모란이 뚝뚝 떨어져 버린 날
나는 비로소 봄을 여읜 설움에 잠길 테요
오월 어느 날 그 하루 무덥던 날
떨어져 누운 꽃잎마저 시들어 버리고는
천지에 모란은 자취도 없어지고
뻗쳐오르던 내 보람 서운케 무너졌느니
모란이 지고 말면 그뿐 내 한 해는 다 가고 말아
삼백예순날 하냥 섭섭해 우옵내다
모란이 피기까지는
나는 아직 기다리고 있을 테요 찬란한 슬픔의 봄을

Until Peonies Bloom

Until peonies bloom

I just go on waiting for my spring to come.

On the days when peonies drop, drop their petals,

I finally languish in sorrow at the loss of spring.

One day in May, one sultry day

when the fallen petals have all withered away

and there is no trace of peonies in all the world,

my soaring fulfillment crumbles into irrepressible sorrow.

Once the peonies have finished blooming, my year is done;

for three hundred and sixty gloomy days I sadly lament.

Until peonies bloom

I just go on waiting for a spring of glorious sorrow.

두견(杜鵑)

울어 피를 뱉고 뱉은 피 도로 삼켜
평생을 원한과 슬픔에 지친 작은 새
너는 너른 세상에 설움을 피로 새기러 오고
네 눈물은 수천 세월을 끊임없이 흘려 놓았다
여기는 먼 남쪽 땅 너 쫓겨 숨음 직한 외딴 곳
달빛 너무도 황홀하여 후젓한 이 새벽을
송기한 네 울음 천 길 바다 밑 고기를 놀래이고
하늘가 어린 별들 버르르 떨리겠구나

몇 해라 이 삼경에 빙빙 도는 눈물을
숫지는 못하고 고인 그대로 흘리었느니
서럽고 외롭고 여윈 이 몸은
퍼붓는 네 술잔에 그만 지늘껴느니
무섬증 드는 이 새벽 가지 울리는 저승의 노래
저기 성 밑을 돌아나가는 죽음의 자랑찬 소리여
달빛 오히려 마음 어둘 저 흰 등 흐느껴 가신다
오래 시들어 파리한 마음마저 가고지워라

비탄의 넋이 붉은 마음만 낱낱 시들피느니
짙은 봄 옥 속 춘향이 아니 죽었을라디야
옛날 왕궁을 나신 나이 어린 임금이
산골에 홀히 우시다 너를 따라 가시었느니
고금도(古今島) 마주 보이는 남쪽 바닷가 한 많은 귀양 길
천리 망아지 얼렁 소리 쉰 듯 멈추고
선비 여윈 얼굴 푸른 물에 띄웠을 제
네 한(恨) 된 울음 죽음을 호려 불렀으리라

The Cuckoo

Little bird, weary of a lifetime in rancor and sorrow,
you cough blood after singing, then swallow it again;
you came to this world to delve deep into sorrow by blood,
your tears have endlessly clouded a myriad ages.
This southern region is secluded, you can hide in exile.
The moonlight is so dazzling, this desolate dawn,
your anguish startles fish a thousand leagues under the sea,
makes infant stars at the sky's edge shudder.

Tears pooling and pooling late at night for so many years
that I could never wash away, they simply pooled and flowed,
and I—sorrowful, lonesome, grieving—
finally grew weary of the wine-glass you kept filling,
songs from the beyond that echo near in this dawn full of fear,
death's boastful voice circling the foot of the city walls.
The moonlight, that pale lantern sobbing to win hearts, is going.
The long-since emaciated, gaunt heart likewise goes.

Since your anguish makes every red heart wither then bloom,
could Chunhyang avoid death in prison in highest spring?
In ancient times a child king set out from the palace,
wept all alone in a mountain valley, then followed you
and on the south coast opposite Gogeum Island, on a bitter homeward path
the sound of a galloping pony came to a halt, wearied
and a scholar's haggard face floated in blue waters
as your regret-filled voice conjured even death.

너 아니 울어도 이 세상 서럽고 쓰린 것을
이른 봄 수풀이 초록빛 들어 풀 내음새 그윽하고
가는 댓잎에 초승달 매달려 애틋한 밝은 어둠을
너 몹시 안타까워 포실거리며 훗훗 목메었느니
아니 울고는 하마 지고 없으리 오! 불행의 넋이여
우지진 진달래 와직 지우는 이 삼경의 네 울음
희미한 줄 산(山)이 살폿 물러서고
조그만 시골이 흥청 깨어진다

1935: 물 내음새 > 풀 내음새.

Without your song, this world is so sorrowful, so wracked;

early in spring as the groves become green, the grass is fragrant;

seeing the pitiful bright darkness as the crescent moon hangs from slender bamboo leaves

you tremble, on the verge of tears, feeling pity;

if you did not sing, you would surely die, oh, anguished spirit.

You call late at night when thick-clustered azalea flowers fall

and gently vague mountain ranges draw back,

little villages suddenly wake.

1935, 2nd line of the last section: the water is fragrant.

Note: The name of the bird evoked in this poem is usually translated "cuckoo" although "nightingale" might be more suitable as it is heard by night. Its plaintive song is said to be the lament of the spirit of a former ruler of China's Shu kingdom who died in exile and longs to return to his lost kingdom. Gogeum Island lies just off the coast close to Gangjin, the poet's home. In times past it often served as a place of banishment for scholars exiled from Seoul for political reasons. Chunhyang is the heroine of a tale of faithful love; the scholar she loves has gone to Seoul to pursue his career but she promises to wait for him; a cruel magistrate has her imprisoned when she refuses to submit to his desire. In most versions, there is a happy ending but in another poem, Kim Yeong-Nang suggests that she died in prison.

청명 (淸明)

호르 호르르 호르르르 가을 아침
취어진 청명을 마시며 거닐면
수풀이 호르르 벌레가 호르르르
청명은 내 머릿속 가슴 속을 젖어 들어
발 끝 손 끝으로 새어 나가나니

온 살결 터럭 끝은 모두 눈이요 입이라
나는 수풀의 정을 알 수 있고
벌레의 예지를 알 수 있다
그리하여 나도 이 아침 청명의
가장 고읍지 못한 노래꾼이 된다

수풀과 벌레는 자고 깨인 어린애라
밤새워 빨고도 이슬은 남았다
남았거든 나를 주라
나는 이 청명에도 주리나니
방에 문을 달고 벽을 향해 숨 쉬지 않았느뇨

햇발이 처음 쏟아오아
청명은 갑자기 으리으리한 관을 쓴다
그때에 토록 하고 동백 한 알은 빠지나니
오! 그 빛남 그 고요함
간밤에 하늘을 쫓긴 별살의 흐름이 저러했다

Brightness

Gulping, gulping, I drink down the autumn morning.
I walk along intoxicated, absorbing the brightness.
As I gulp down the bushes, gulp the insects,
the brightness penetrates my head, my heart,
then slips away through my feet and fingertips.

My skin's every hair is eye, mouth.
I can sense each bush's affection,
can sense each insect's wisdom.
With that I become this morning's
most unlovely serenader.

Bushes and insects are children waking from sleep;
there is still dew left, though they suckled all night.
Give me some too, since some remains.
I hunger after this brightness.
I have been in my room, door shut, breathing at the walls.

As the first ray of sunshine comes bursting through
the brightness suddenly puts on a kingly crown.
Just then, *plop*, a camellia seed falls.
Oh! Such splendor, such stillness.
Just like last night's flow of starlight expelled from the sky.

온 소리의 앞 소리요
온 빛깔의 비롯이라
이 청명에 포근 취어진 내 마음
감각의 낯익은 고향을 찾았노라
평생 못 떠날 내 집을 들었노라

1935 마지막 2줄:
"감각의 낯익은 고향을 차젓노라
평생 못떠날 내집을 드럿노라."

Sound preceding every sound,

origin of every hue,

warmly refreshed by this brightness, my heart

is just one blade of grass growing in a cool vale of feeling,

one grub spending a lifetime drenched in dew.

1935 the last two lines read:

"has found the familiar home of feeling,

has entered the house it will never leave again."

황홀한 달빛

황홀한 달빛
바다는 은(銀)장
천지는 꿈인 양
이리 고요하다

부르면 내려올 듯
정뜬 달은
맑고 은은한 노래
울려날 듯

저 은장 위에
떨어진단들
달이야 설마
깨어질라고

떨어져 보라
저 달 어서 떨어져라
그 혼란스럼
아름다운 천동 지동

후젓한 삼경(三更)
산 위에 홀히
꿈꾸는 바다
깨울 수 없다

Intoxicating Moonlight

In the intoxicating moonlight
the sea is a sheet of silver;
heaven and earth lie so still,
just like a dream.

The familiar moon
seems ready to come down if called,
it seems ready to give voice
to a pure, resonant song.

Suppose it came falling down
onto that sheet of silver?
Surely the moon
could not shatter there?

Fall then,
moon, fall away—
that confusion, that beautiful noise,
that shaking of heaven and earth,

in deep forlorn night
on the mountain top,
could not waken
the lonely dreaming sea.

마당 앞 맑은 새암을

마당 앞
맑은 새암을 들여다본다

저 깊은 땅 밑에
사로잡힌 넋 있어
언제나 먼 하늘만
내어다보고 계심 같아

별이 총총한
맑은 새암을 들여다본다

저 깊은 땅속에
편히 누운 넋 있어
이 밤 그 눈 반짝이고
그의 겉몸 부르심 같아

마당 앞
맑은 새암은 내 영혼의 얼굴

The Clear Well in Front of the Yard

I gaze into the clear well
in front of the yard.

Deep beneath the ground
there is a soul imprisoned.
It seems always to be looking down
at the distant sky.

I gaze into the clear well
where stars cluster thick.

Deep within that ground
there is a soul lying peacefully.
This evening its eyes are sparkling
like a call to its outward body.

That clear well
in front of the yard is my soul's face.

사행시 Quatrains

뵈지도 않는 입김

뵈지도 않는 입김의 가는 실마리
새파란 하늘 끝에 오름과 같이
대숲의 숨은 마음 기여 찾으려
삶은 오로지 바늘 끝같이

님 두시고 가는 길의

님 두시고 가는 길의 애끈한 마음이여
한숨 쉬면 꺼질 듯한 조매로운 꿈길이여
이 밤은 캄캄한 어느 뉘 시골인가
이슬같이 고인 눈물을 손끝으로 깨치나니

무너진 성터에

무너진 성터에 바람이 세나니
가을은 쓸쓸한 맛뿐이구려
희끗 희끗 산국화 나부끼면서
가을은 애닯다 속삭이느뇨

저녁때 저녁때

저녁때 저녁때 외로운 마음
붙잡지 못하여 걸어 다님을
누구라 불어 주신 바람이기로
눈물을 눈물을 빼앗아 가오

Unseen Breath

Like a fine thread of unseen breath
rising to the farthest ends of an azure sky,
life is like nothing so much as a needle's point
in search of a bamboo grove's hidden heart.

Setting Off After Leaving My Love

Sorrowful of heart, I set off after leaving my love,
down a fragile dream path that might vanish if once I sigh.
Whose dark village can this night be?
I mar with my fingertips tears that pool like dew

Over Ruined City Walls

Over ruined city walls the wind blows strong,
autumn only seems more desolate.
White-specked chrysanthemums flutter
as the autumn whispers, broken-hearted.

At Evening, at Evening

At evening, at evening, unable to master
my lonely heart, I go walking.
Someone is sending a wind
that robs me of tear after tear.

풀 위에 맺어지는

풀 위에 맺어지는 이슬을 본다
눈썹에 아롱지는 눈물을 본다
풀 위엔 정기가 꿈같이 오르고
가슴은 간곡히 입을 벌인다

푸른 향물 흘러 버린

푸른 향물 흘러 버린 언덕 위에
내 마음 하루살이 나래로다
보실보실 가을 눈이 그 나래를 치며
허공의 속삭임을 들으라 한다

좁은 길가에

좁은 길가에 무덤이 하나
이슬에 젖이우며 밤을 새인다
나는 사라져 저 별이 되오리
뫼 아래 누워서 희미한 별을

허리띠 매는 새악시

허리띠 매는 새악시 마음실 같이
꽃가지에 은은한 그늘이 지면
흰날의 내 가슴 아지랑이 낀다
흰날의 내 가슴 아지랑이 낀다

Pearling over Grass

I see dew pearling over grass,
I see tears speckling eyebrows.
Over the grass vitality rises like a dream
and my heart lies open in yearning.

Blue Fragrance Has Faded

On a hill from where summer's blue fragrance has faded
my heart is a dayfly's wings.
Lightly falling autumn rain-eyes shake those wings,
saying : listen to the whispering air.

Beside a Narrow Path

Beside a narrow path, one grave
stays awake all night long, soaked by dew.
Once I am dead I'll become a star,
a faint star, as I lie in the grave.

A Girl Tying Her Sash

As dim autumn settles on flowering branches
like the mind of a girl tying her sash,
haze wraps round my bright heart,
haze wraps round my bright heart

못 오실 임이 그리웁기로

못 오실 임이 그리웁기로
흩어진 꽃잎이 슬프랬던가
빈손 쥐고 오신 봄이 거저나 가시련만
흘러가는 눈물이면 님의 마음 젖이련만

다정히도 불어오는

다정히도 불어오는 바람이길래
내 숨결 가부엽게 실어 보냈오
하늘가를 스치고 휘도는 바람
어이면 한숨만 몰아다 주오

향내 없다고 버리시려면

향내 없다고 버리시려면
내 목숨 꺾지나 마르시오
외로운 들꽃은 들 가에 시들어
철없는 그이의 발끝에 조을

어덕에 누워

어덕에 누워 바다를 보면
빛나는 잔물결 헤일 수 없지만
눈만 감으면 떠오는 얼굴
뵈올 적마다 꼭 한 분이구려

Longing for My Lover Who Cannot Come

Are the scattered petals telling me I should feel sad,
longing for my lover who cannot come?
Though spring came empty-handed, and now has gone,
as tears flowed, that lover's heart was drenched.

Blowing Affectionately

Lightly I sent forth a breath
like a wind blowing affectionately
but the roaming wind, after skimming the sky,
only brought me back a sigh.

Discarded for Having No Fragrance

If you are going to discard it for having no fragrance,
I beg you, do not pluck my life.
A lonely flower, withering along the edge of the fields,
should go on sleeping till trampled by rough feet.

When I Lie on a Hill

When I lie on a hill and gaze at the sea
I cannot count the shining ripples one by one.
Yet if I close my eyes, the face that comes to mind
is always the selfsame face, every time I see it.

밤사람 그립고야

밤사람 그립고야
말없이 걸어가는 밤사람 그립고야
보름 넘은 달 그리매 마음아이 서어로와
오랜 밤을 나도 혼자 밤사람 그립고야

눈물 속 빛나는 보람과

눈물 속 빛나는 보람과 웃음 속 어둔 슬픔은
오직 가을 하늘에 떠도는 구름
다만 후젓하고 줄 데 없는 마음만 예나 이제나
외론 밤 바람 숫긴 찬 별을 보랐습니다

빈 포케트에

빈 포케트에 손 찌르고 폴 베를레느 찾는 날
온몸은 흐렁흐렁 눈물도 찔끔 했노라
오! 비가 이리 쭐쭐쭐 내리는 날은
설운 소리 한 천 마디 외었으면 싶어라

바람에 나부끼는 깔잎

바람에 나부끼는 깔잎
여울에 희롱하는 깔잎
알 만 모를 만 숨 쉬고 눈물 맺은
내 청춘의 어느 날 서러운 손짓이여

I Yearn for a Nighttime Companion!

I yearn for a nighttime companion!
I yearn for a nighttime companion who walks without speaking.
Shadows cast by the waning moon so grieve my heart
alone on long nights that I yearn for a nighttime companion.

The Bright Recompense in Tears

The bright recompense in tears, the dark sorrow in laughter
are merely clouds drifting in an autumn sky.
Then as now my silent, lonesome heart gazed
at the icy stars caressed by the lonely wind.

I Thrust My Hand into an Empty Pocket

On days when I thrust my hand into an empty pocket in quest of Paul Verlaine
my whole body is sad and tears flow
but, ah, on days when rain falls on and on
I long to utter a thousand sorrowful words.

Reeds Trembling in the Breeze

Reeds trembling in the breeze,
reeds frolicking in rapids,
sorrowful gestures of my youthful days,
knowing, not knowing, sad tearful days.

뻘은 가슴을

뻘은 가슴을 훤히 벗고
개풀 수줍어 고개 숙이네
한낮에 배란 놈이 저 가슴 만졌구나
뻘건 맨발로는 나도 자꾸 간지럽구나

그 밖에 더 아실 이

그 밖에 더 아실 이 안 계실거나
그이의 젖은 옷깃 눈물이라고
빛나는 별 아래 애닯은 입김이
이슬로 맺히고 맺히었음을

밤이면 고총 아래

밤이면 고총 아래 고개 숙이고
낮이면 하늘 보고 웃음 좀 웃고
너른 들 쓸쓸하여 외론 할미꽃
아무도 몰래 지는 새벽 지친 별

저 곡조만

저 곡조만 마저 호동글 사라지면
목 속의 구슬을 물 속에 버리려니
해와 같이 떴다 지는 구름 속 종달은
새날 또 새론 섬 새 구슬 머금고 오리

Mudflats Brightly Bare Their Breasts

Mudflats brightly bare their breasts,
the sedges bashfully bow their heads.
In broad daylight one cheeky boat dares touch those breasts
while I shamelessly keep tickling them with my bare feet.

How Could Anyone Else Know

How could anyone else know
that flowing tears had soaked his collar?
In the bright starlight his anguished breath
was condensing, condensing as dew.

In the Lee of an Old Grave by Night

Bowing its head in the lee of an old grave by night,
looking up at the sky with a slight smile by day,
the wide fields being desolate, the pasqueflower is lonely
as the weary stars fade at dawn, unnoticed by anyone.

If Its Melody

If its melody should ever vanish completely,
the skylark will spit the jewel in its throat into the sea.
Then tomorrow, in clouds that rise and set with the sun,
it will return, bearing in its beak a new jewel from a new island.

산골을 놀이터로

산골을 놀이터로 커난 새악시
가슴속은 구슬같이 맑으련마는
바라뵈는 먼 곳이 그리움인지
동이인 채 산길에 섰기도 하네

사랑은 깊으기

사랑은 깊으기 푸른 하늘
맹세는 가볍기 흰 구름 쪽
그 구름 사라진다 서럽지는 않으나
그 하늘 큰 조화 못 믿지는 않으나

빠른 철로에

빠른 철로에 조는 손님아
이 시골 이 정거장 행여 잊을라
한가하고 그립고 쓸쓸한 시골 사람의
드나드는 이 정거장 행여 잊을라

숲 향기 숨길을

숲 향기 숨길을 가로막았소
발끝에 구슬이 깨이어지고
달 따라 들길을 걸어 다니다
하룻밤 여름을 새워 버렸소

A Valley for Her Playground

A young girl who grew up with a valley for her playground
has a heart as pure as any jewel.
Yet here she is standing on a mountain path, a water pot balanced on her head.
Perhaps she is longing for a place she can see far away.

Love Is as Deep

Love is as deep as a blue sky,
its promises are light as a little white cloud.
I am not upset though the cloud disappears,
still I believe in the sky's great harmony, yet . . .

On an Express Train

Passenger dozing on an express train,
you should not forget this rural station,
this station frequented by rural folk,
relaxed, homesick, so desolate.

The Forest's Fragrance Took My Breath Away

The forest's fragrance took my breath away
as gems shattered beneath my feet.
I walked across the fields following the moon
all night long, unsleeping through the summer.

그 색시 서럽다

그 색시 서럽다 그 얼굴 그 동자가
가을 하늘가에 도는 바람 숫긴 구름조각
핼쑥하고 서느라워 어디로 떠갔으랴
그 색시 서럽다 옛날의 옛날의

떠 날아가는 마음의

떠 날아가는 마음의 파름한 길을
꿈이런가 눈감고 헤아리려니
가슴에 선뜻 빛깔이 돌아
생각을 끊으며 눈물 고이며

미움이란 말 속에

미움이란 말 속에 보기 싫은 아픔
미움이란 말 속에 하잔한 뉘우침
그러나 그 말씀 씹히고 씹힐 때
한 까풀 넘치어 흐르는 눈물

생각하면 부끄러운

생각하면 부끄러운 일이어라
석가나 예수같이 큰일을 하리라고
내 가슴에 불덩이가 타오르던 때
학생이란 피로 싸인 부끄러운 때

온몸을 감도는

온몸을 감도는 붉은 핏줄이
꼭 감긴 눈 속에 뭉치어 있네
날랜 소리 한마디 날랜 칼 하나
그 핏줄 딱 끊어 버릴 수 없나

That Girl Is Sorrowful

That girl is mournful, her face, her eyes.
One little cloud goes past, blown by the wind in the autumn sky.
Pallid and forlorn, whither did it go?
That girl is mournful, the girl of bygone, bygone days.

My Drifting Mind

Eyes closed, I attempt to fathom the pale blue path
of my drifting mind. Is this a dream?
In my breast a bright light shines,
abolishing thought, pooling tears.

Within the Word Hatred

Within the word hatred, unwelcome pain,
within the word hatred, trivial repentance,
but when I keep chewing the word,
tears overflow.

I Feel Ashamed When I Remember the Days

I feel ashamed when I remember the days
when my heart used to be ablaze
with ideas of doing great deeds, like the Buddha or Jesus,
shameful days enveloped in student blood.

Circling My Body

The crimson blood vessels circling my body
are all united in my tightly shut eyes.
Could not one sharp word or one sharp sword
sever them at a single blow?

Poems 1938–1940

거문고

검은 벽에 기대선 채로
해가 스무 번 바뀌었는데
내 기린(麒麟)은 영영 울지를 못한다

그 가슴을 통 흔들고 간 노인의 손
지금 어느 끝없는 향연에 높이 앉았으려니
땅위의 외론 기린이야 하마 잊어졌을라

바깥은 거친 들 이리 떼만 몰려다니고
사람인 양 꾸민 잔나비 떼들 쏘다 다니어
내 기린은 맘 둘 곳 몸 둘 곳 없어지다

문 아주 굳이 닫고 벽에 기대선 채
해가 또 한 번 바뀌거늘
이 밤도 내 기린은 맘 놓고 울들 못한다

A Geomungo

While the year has changed twenty times
my kirin has stayed leaning against the black wall,
never able to sing.

The hand of the old man that once plucked at its heart
now occupies a lofty place in endless banquets above,
while you, lonely kirin, here below, how could you be forgotten?

Outside are wild lands where packs of wolves roam,
groups of apes gambol, only seemingly human,
so there is nowhere my kirin can lay its heart, rest its body.

Once more the year has changed,
and, still leaning against the wall, the door shut tight,
tonight again my kirin is unable to sing freely.

Note: The *geomungo* (here identified with the mythical kirin) is a six-stringed Korean instrument very similar to the *gayageum*, but the strings are plucked with a plectrum. It was an instrument favored by Korean scholars. The kirin is a mythical creature with hoofs and horns and the head of a chimera, found throughout East Asia. It can walk on grass yet not trample the blades, and it can also walk on water. It is normally gentle but becomes fierce if a pure person is threatened by someone wicked. The wolves and apes in the poem are images of the Japanese occupying Korea, and those Koreans who imitate them.

가야금

북으로
북으로
울고 간다 기러기

남방의
대숲 밑
뉘 휘어 날켰느뇨

앞서고 뒤섰다
어지럴 리 없으나

가냘픈 실오라기
네 목숨이 조매로아

A Gayageum

Northward,

northward

they fly calling, the geese.

Who sent you flying off

from beneath the bamboo groves

of the south?

Forward or backward,

no sign of disorder.

Slender strings,

your life is so full of suspense.

Note: The *gayageum* is a twelve-stringed instrument similar to the *geomungo*; the strings are plucked with the fingers.

빛깔 환히

빛깔 환히
동창에 떠오름을 기다리신가
아흐레 어린 달이
부름도 없이 홀로 났네
월출동령(月出東嶺)!
팔도사람 다 맞이하소
기척없이 따르는 마음
그대나 홀히 싸안아 주오

원래제목 : 달맞이

A Ray of Light

Are you waiting for a ray of light

to rise bright beyond the east window?

The infant moon of the month's ninth day

has risen alone, unsummoned.

The moon is rising over the eastern hills.

Countrymen, welcome it!

You should speedily embrace

the hearts that follow without a sign.

Original title: "Moon-Gazing."

연 1

내 어린 날!
아슬한 하늘에 뜬 연같이
바람에 깜박이는 연실같이
내 어린 날! 아슨풀하다

하늘은 파랗고 끝없고
편편한 연실은 조매롭고
오! 흰 연 그새에 높이
아실아실 떠 놀다 내 어린 날!

바람 일어 끊어지던 날
엄마 아빠 부르고 울다
희끗희끗한 실낱이 서러워
아침 저녁 나무 밑에 울다

오! 내 어린 날 하얀 옷 입고
외로이 자랐다 하얀 넋 담고
조마조마 길가에 붉은 발자욱
자욱마다 눈물이 고이었었다

Kite 1

My childhood days!
Like a kite floating in the lofty sky,
like a kite-string jerking in the wind,
my childhood days! Far-away days.

So blue the sky, endless,
the kite-string taut;
oh! the white kite so high above,
frolicking in play, my childhood days!

One day the wind rose and snapped the string.
I wept, called out: Mama, Papa!
The scrap of grizzled string seemed sad
as, morning and evening, I wept beneath the tree.

Ah! Wearing the white clothes of my childhood days
I grew up in solitude, bearing a white soul,
nervous at red footprints along the roadside
with tears pooling in every footprint.

오 월

들길은 마을에 들자 붉어지고
마을 골목은 들로 내려서자 푸르러진다
바람은 넘실 천 이랑 만 이랑
이랑 이랑 햇빛이 갈라지고
보리도 허리통이 부끄럽게 드러났다
꾀꼬리는 여태 혼자 날아볼 줄 모르나니
암컷이라 쫓길 뿐
수놈이라 쫓을 뿐
황금 빛난 길이 어지럴 뿐
얇은 단장하고 아양 가득 차 있는
산봉우리야 오늘 밤 너 어디로 가버리련?

May

On entering the village, field paths turn red
while the village alleys, descending to the fields, become green.
The wind billows in a thousand furrows, ten thousand,
sunlight shatters dazzlingly there.
The barley has developed a shamefully conspicuous girth.
At present no oriole is capable of flying alone,
the female is ever pursued,
the male ever pursuing.
The paths shine golden, ever more dizzying.
Lightly made-up, utterly coquettish
mountain peaks, where are you off to tonight?

독을 차고

내 가슴에 독을 찬 지 오래로다
아직 아무도 해한 일 없는 새로 뽑은 독
벗은 그 무서운 독 그만 흩어 버리라 한다
나는 그 독이 선뜻 벗도 해할지 모른다 위협하고

독 안 차고 살아도 머지않아 너 나 마저 가 버리면
누억천만 (屢億千萬) 세대가 그 뒤로 잠자코 흘러가고
나중에 땅덩이 모지라져 모래알이 될 것임을
"허무한데!" 독은 차서 무엇 하느냐고?

아! 내 세상에 태어났음을 원망 않고 보낸
어느 하루가 있었던가 "허무한데!" 허나
앞뒤로 덤비는 이리 승냥이 바야흐로 내 마음을 노리매
내 산 채 짐승의 밥이 되어 찢기우고 할퀴우라 내맡긴 신세임을

나는 독을 품고 선선히 가리라
마감 날 내 외로운 혼 건지기 위하여

Carrying Poison

I have long carried poison in my breast,
newly drawn poison that so far has harmed nobody.
A friend tells me I should pour away that dreadful poison.
I threaten: that poison might suddenly harm even my friend.

Even if our lives are not full of poison, very soon you and I will have gone for good,
then a trillion generations will flow away in silence,
ultimately the earth will wear away to a grain of sand.
Such things are all vanity! Why be full of poison?

Ah! Was there one single day that I spent without resenting
having been born in this world? All vanity, I say.
Before and behind me, wolves, coyotes rush for my heart.
My destiny is to be eaten alive by beasts, to be torn apart, clawed.

Bearing poison still, I will readily go,
to save my lonely soul on the last day of my life.

묘비명

생전에 이다지 외로운 사람
어이해 뫼 아래 빗돌 세우오
초조론 길손의 한숨이라도
해어진 고충에 자주 떠오리
날마다 외롭다 가고 말 사람
그래도 뫼 아래 빗돌 세우리
"외롭건 내 곁에 쉬시다 가라"
한(恨) 되는 한 마디 사기실는가

Memorial

What can be the point of setting a stone

above the grave of someone who was so lonely in life?

Would fretful travelers bother even to sigh

at the sight of an old, dilapidated grave?

Still, set up a stone before the grave

of one who was every day lonely, till he died.

"If you feel lonely, rest here beside me a while."

What if you carved on it some such bitter-sounding words?

한줌 흙

본시 평탄했을 마음 아니로다
굳이 톱질하여 산산 찢어 놓았다

풍경이 눈을 홀리지 못하고
사랑이 생각을 흐리지 못한다

지쳐 원망도 않고 산다

대체 내 노래는 어디로 갔느냐
가장 거룩한 것 이 눈물만

앗인 마음 끝내 못 빼앗고
주린 마음 끄득 못 배불리고

어차피 몸도 피로워졌다
바삐 관에 못을 다져라

아무려나 한줌 흙이 되는구나

A Handful of Dust

From the start my heart was not destined for composure.
It was harshly hacked and rent apart.

Landscapes never fascinate my eyes,
love cannot trouble my thoughts.

Weary, I live without resentment.

What could have become of my songs?
The most sacred things are just these tears.

To the end I could never enthrall my dissatisfied heart,
could never fill my hungry heart.

Nonetheless, my body fell ill.
Quickly, nail my coffin shut.

In any case, I am destined to become a handful of dust.

강물

잠 자리 설워서 일어났소
꿈이 고읍지 못해 눈을 떴소

베개에 차단히 눈물은 젖었는데
흐르다 못해 한 방울 애끈히 고이었소

꿈에 본 강물이라 몹시 보고 싶었소
무럭무럭 김 오르며 내리는 강물

언덕을 혼자서 거니노라니
물오리 갈매기도 끼륵끼륵

강물을 철철 흘러가면서
아심찮이 그 꿈도 떠싣고 갔소

꿈이 아닌 생시 가진 설움도
자꾸 강물은 떠싣고 갔소

A River

Too sorrowful as I slept, I woke.
My dream was not sweet, so I opened my eyes.

The pillow was moist with icy tears;
they flowed fast, then one drop lingered, forlorn.

I longed to see the river I had glimpsed in my dream,
a river steaming as it flowed.

As I walked alone over the hill,
ducks and geese were calling.

The river flowed on, brimming full,
and fortunately it bore my dream away.

The sorrow I felt, in dream and waking,
the river took and bore it away.

한길에 누워

팔다리 쭉 뻗고 한길에 펑 드러눕다
총총 배긴 별이 방울지듯 치렁치렁
찬란(燦爛)만 저리 유구(悠久)했다

사람아 왜 나를 귀찮게 흔들기냐
기껏해야 용수 같은 내 토굴 찾아들려고

한창 새벽 '해'와 '길'이 쓸 곳 없다
찬란만 저리 유구코나
내 기원도 세기를 넘어설까

세월이 감격을 좀먹길래
밤마다 주령(酒靈)을 졸라댔다

그래 사람들아 그렇게들 얌전키냐
하나도 서럽잖고 두 번 원통치도 않아
어린 자식 앉혀 놓고 똑바른 말 못 할테냐

그때 열두 담장 못 넘어뛰고 만
그 선비는 차라리 목마른 체 사약을 받았니라고

Lying in the Middle of the Road

I am lying in the very middle of the road, arms and legs spreadeagled.
The clustered twinkling stars hang like bells.
Their splendor alone is eternal.

Why are people shaking me so annoyingly?
Do they want me back in my wine-strainer-like cave?

There is nowhere to write "sun" and "road."
Their splendor alone is eternal.
I wonder if my prayer will last for centuries.

Time leaves feelings moth-eaten,
so why have you been pestering me about the way I drink every evening?

Right, all of you, are you so genteel?
Not a bit unhappy, nor the least bit resentful,
can't you set your kids down and do some straight talking?

In the old days, a gentleman unable to leap over twelve walls
is said to have been sent poison to drink in his thirst.

우감 (偶感)

우렁찬 소리 한 마디 안 그리운가
내 비위에 꼭 맞는 그 한 마디!
입에 돌고 귀에 아직 우는구나

40 가찬 나이, 내 일찍 나서 좋다
창자가 짤리는 설움도 맛봐서 좋다
간 쓸개가 가까스로 남았거늘

아버지도 싫다 너무 이른 때 나셨다
아들도 싫다 너무 지나서 나왔다
내 나이 알맞다 가장 서럽게 자랐다

행복을 찾노라 모두들 환장한다
제 혼자 때문만 아니라는구나 주제넘게 남의 행복까지!
갖다 부처님께 바쳐라 앓는 마누라나 달래라

봄 되면 우렁찬 소리 여기저기 나는 듯 해 자지러지다가도
거저 되살아날 듯싶다만 내 보금자리는 한양 서런 행복이 가득 차 있다

A Sudden Feeling

I yearn to pronounce one word in a resonant voice.
That one word just right for my mood!
After passing the lips, still it rings in my ears.

A full forty years old, I am glad I was born early.
I am glad I have experienced heartbreaking sorrow.
I myself have barely survived.

I dislike the way my father was born too early,
I dislike the way my son was born too late.
I am the right age, I grew up most sorrowfully.

Everyone's crazy about finding happiness.
Not only for themselves alone, they say, but, beyond all limits, even others' happiness too!
Go offer that to Buddha! Comfort your sick wife.

When spring comes, I cower as resonant voices seem to arise here and there;
then I have a feeling that I am simply alive again, while my home is full of sorrowful happiness.

내 훗진 노래

그대 내 훗진 노래를 들으실까
꽃은 가득 피고 벌떼 닝닝거리고

그대 내 그늘 없는 소리를 들으실까
안개 자욱이 푸른 골을 다 덮었네

그대 내 흥 안 이는 노래를 들으실까
봄 물결은 왜 이는지 출렁거린데

내 소리는 깨벗어 봄철이 싫다리
호젓한 소리 가다가는 씁쓸한 소리

어슨 달밤 빨간 동백꽃 쥐어 따서
마음씨 냥 꽁꽁 주물러 버리네

원래제목 : 호젓한 노래

My Solitary Song

Would you care to hear my solitary song?
Flowers are in full bloom, bees buzz in clusters.

Would you care to hear my shadowless song?
Fog has thickly covered all the green valley.

Would you care to hear my lifeless song?
Spring waves ripple for no reason.

My voice is a naked springtime,
a solitary voice, a bitter voice along the way.

On misty nights, plucking a crimson camellia,
I crush it as if it were a seed of my heart.

Original title: "Solitary Song."

춘향

큰칼 쓰고 옥에 든 춘향이는
제 마음이 그리도 독했던가 놀래었다
성문이 부서져도 이 악물고
사또를 노려보던 교만한 눈
그는 옛날 성학사(成學士) 박팽년이
불 지짐에도 태연하였음을 알았었니라
오! 일편단심

원통코 독한 마음 잠과 꿈을 이뤘으랴
옥방 첫날 밤은 길고도 무서워라
설움이 사무치고 지쳐 쓰러지면
남강의 외론 혼은 불리어 나왔느니
논개! 어린 춘향을 꼭 안어
밤새워 마음과 살을 어루만지다
오! 일편단심

사랑이 무엇이기
정절이 무엇이기
그 때문에 꽃의 춘향 그만 옥사하단 말가
지네 구렁이 같은 변학도의
흉측한 얼굴에 까무러쳐도
어린 가슴 달큼히 지켜주는 도련님 생각
오! 일편단심

Chunhyang

Chunhyang was amazed at her own tenacity
as she was taken to prison with a great cangue round her neck.
Those proud eyes that glared at the magistrate,
her teeth clenched, come what may!
She recalled the great scholar Bak Peng-nyeon of ancient times,
his unshaken calm despite torture by red-hot irons.
Ah, such singleness of heart!

With a heart so chagrined and resolute, how could she dream?
So fearful that first long night in prison must have seemed!
When she collapsed, overcome with sorrow,
the solitary soul from the Nam River came at her bidding,
Nongae! She embraced tightly youthful Chunhyang,
consoling her in body and soul all the night long.
Ah, such singleness of heart!

Such love!
Such devotion!
Should lovely Chunhyang die in prison on their account?
When she was about to faint at the hideous face
of that slimy centipede Pyeon Hakdo,
came the memory of her young master, preserved in her heart.
Ah, such singleness of heart!

상하고 멍든 자리 마디마디 문지르며
눈물은 타고 남은 간을 젖어 내렸다
버들잎이 창살에 선뜻 스치는 날도
도련님 말방울 소리는 아니 들렸다
삼경을 새우다가 그는 고만 단장(斷腸)하다
두견이 울어 두견이 울어 남원 고을도 깨어지고
오! 일편단심

깊은 겨울밤 비바람은 우루루루
피 칠해 논 옥 창살을 들이치는데
옥 죽음한 원귀들이 구석구석에 휙휙 울어
청절(淸節) 춘향도 혼을 잃고 몸을 버려 버렸다
밤새도록 까무러치고
해 돋을 녘 깨어나다
오! 일편단심

믿고 바라고 눈 아프게 보고 싶던 도련님이
죽기 전에 와 주셨다 춘향은 살았구나
쑥대머리 귀신 얼굴 된 춘향이 보고
이 도령은 잔인스레 웃었다 저 때문의 정절이 자랑스러워
"우리 집이 팍 망해서 상거지가 되었지야."
틀림없는 도련님 춘향은 원망도 안 했니라
오! 일편단심

모진 춘향이 그 밤 새벽에 또 까무러쳐서는
영 다시 깨어나진 못했었다 두견은 울었건만
도련님 다시 뵈어 한을 풀었으나 살아날 가망은 아주 끊기고

Until Peonies Bloom

As she rubbed every wound and bruise,
tears fell, refreshing her anguished heart,
but even on days when willow leaves stroked her window
no sound could be heard of her love's horse-bells.
Staying awake till late at night, she grew heartbroken.
The cuckoo sobbed, the cuckoo sobbed, all Namwon woke.
Ah, such singleness of heart!

As a storm raged wild one winter's night
beating at the blood-smeared prison bars
while the ghosts of those who had died in prison screamed,
faithful Chunhyang lost her senses, fell to the floor.
She lay in a faint all through the night
then awoke as the sun was rising.
Ah, such singleness of heart!

The young master she trusted, hoped for, ardently longed to see,
arrived before she died. Chunhyang was saved.
At the sight of phantom-faced Chunhyang
Yi Doryeong laughed bitterly. He was proud of her devotion:
"Our family was ruined, I became a beggar," he lied.
Chunhyang did not blame her faithful love at all.
Ah, such singleness of heart!

Wretched Chunhyang collapsed again early the next day
and never woke again. The cuckoo called in vain.
She had seen her love, so no bitterness remained

온몸 푸른 맥도 홱 풀려 버렸을 법
출두 끝에 어사는 춘향의 몸을 거두며 울다
"내 변가(卞哥)보다 잔인 무지하여 춘향을 죽였구나."
오! 일편단심

but she believed there was no hope that she could be saved, so her body lost all its vital powers.

After revealing his identity, the secret inspector weeps, holding Chunhyang's body.

"Crueler even than wicked Pyeon, I have killed Chunhyang."

Ah, such singleness of heart!

Note: In the well-known tale of Chunhyang, the young aristocrat Yi Doryeong falls in love with Chunhyang, daughter of a gisaeng (female entertainer) living in the town of Namwon. After he leaves for Seoul to take the exam that will qualify him for administrative service, a new magistrate, Pyeon Hakdo, arrives and demands that she submit to him. When she refuses, he has her imprisoned and tortured but she remains faithful though sentenced to death. At last, her love returns as a secret royal inspector, disguised as a beggar. He reveals his identity, Chunhyang is released and the wicked magistrate is punished. In most versions, the lovers live happily for many years. Nongae was a gisaeng who is celebrated for having sacrificed her life to protect Korea during the sixteenth-century Japanese invasion. She is said to have embraced a Japanese general, then dragged him with her over a cliff into a river in Jinju.

집

내 집 아니라
늬 집이라
나르다 얼른 돌아오라
처마 난간이
늬들 가여운 속삭임을 지음(知音)터라

내 집 아니라
늬 집이라
아배 간 뒤 머언 날
아들 손자 잠도 깨우리
문틈 사이 늬는 몇 대(代)째 설워 우느뇨

내 집 아니라
늬 집이라
하늘 날으던 은행잎이
좁은 마루 구석에 품인 듯 안겨든다
태고로 맑은 바람이 거기 살았니라

오! 내 집이라
열 해요 스무 해를
앉았다 누웠달 뿐
문밖에 바쁜 손이
길 잘못 들어 날 찾아오고

손때 살내음도 절었을 난간이
흔히 나를 안고 한가하다
한두 쪽 흰 구름도 사라지는데
한 두엇 저질러 논 부끄러운 짓
파아란 하늘처럼 아슴풀하다

A House

This is not my house,

it's your house.

Quickly come flying back.

The railings round the eaves

are well acquainted with your pitiful whisperings.

This is not my house,

it's your house.

Long after your father left,

you keep on weeping, you might wake your sons and grandchildren.

You keep on weeping, generations later, through the crack of the door.

This is not my house,

it's your house.

Lightly flying gingko leaves

nestle in the corner of the porch as on a breast.

The clear wind has been living there since ancient times.

Ah! Yet this is my house too!

For ten years, twenty years

I have simply sat down, laid down in it.

If a busy visitor knocks at the door

he is visiting only because he has lost his way.

The railings thick with ancient hands' dirt and bodies' smell

embrace me often, empty now.

A few white clouds disappear beyond distant hills,

a few botched, shameful deeds

linger on, faint as the blue sky.

Poems 1946–1950

북

자네 소리하게 내 북을 잡지

진양조 중모리 중중모리
엇모리 잦아지다 휘모라 보아

이렇게 숨결이 꼭 맞아서만 이룬 일이란
인생(人生)에 흔치 않어 어려운 일 시원한 일

소리를 떠나서야 북은 오직 가죽일 뿐
헛 때리면 만갑이도 숨을 고쳐 쉴밖에

장단을 친다는 말이 모자라오
연창(演唱)을 살리는 반주쯤은 지나고
북은 오히려 컨덕터요

떠받는 명고(名鼓)인데 잔가락을 온통 잊으오
떡 궁! 동중정(動中靜)이오 소란 속에 고요 있어
인생이 가을같이 익어 가오

자네 소리하게 내 북을 치지

원래 제 1줄 : 내 북을 치지

Drum

Sing and I will take up my drum.

Using all the rhythms our music offers, slow at first,
then ever faster, I'll beat my drum.

Attaining in this way unity of breathing
is rare in life; it is difficult, exhilarating.

Detached from your singing, my drum is mere leather.
If the beat goes wrong, even the best singer's breathing has to change.

It is not enough to say it beats out rhythms;
more than an accompaniment that supports the singer,
the drum serves rather as conductor.

I am a famous beating drum. Forget all about the little song.
Tack-boom. Quietness in motion, that's me, since there is silence in the midst of uproar,
human life matures like an autumn harvest.

Sing and I will beat my drum.

Original first line: "beat."

바다로 가자

바다로 가자 큰 바다로 가자
우리 인젠 큰 하늘과 넓은 바다를 마음대로 가졌노라
하늘이 바다요 바다가 하늘이라
바다 하늘 모두 다 가졌노라
옳다 그리하여 가슴이 뻐근치야
우리 모두다 가졌구나 큰 바다로 가졌구나

우리는 바다 없이 살았지야 숨막히고 살았지야
그리하여 쪼여 들고 울고불고 하였지야
바다 없는 항구 속에 사로잡힌 몸은
살이 터져나고 뼈 튀겨나고 넋이 흩어지고
하마터면 아주 꺼꾸러져 버릴 것을
오! 바다가 터지도다 큰 바다가 터지도다

쪽배 타면 제주야 가고 오고
독목선(獨木船) 왜 섬이사 갔다 왔지
허나 그게 바달러냐
건너뛰는 실 개천이라
우리 3년 걸려도 큰 배를 짓자꾸나
큰 바다 넓은 하늘을 우리는 가졌노라

우리 큰 배타고 떠나 가자꾸나
창랑을 헤치고 태풍을 걷어차고
하늘과 맞닿은 저 수평선 뚫으리라
큰 호통하고 떠나 가자꾸나
바다 없는 항구에 사로 잡힌 마음들아
툭 털고 일어서자 바다가 네 집이라

Let's Go Down to the Sea

Let's go down to the sea, the vast sea,
for today we possess in freedom the vast sky, the wide sea.
The sky is the sea, the sea is the sky.
We possess both of them fully.
True indeed! Therefore our hearts are heavy.
Let's all go now, let's all go down to the sea.

We have been living suffocating lives without the sea.
Therefore we have been lamenting bitterly our shrunken lives,
our bodies trapped in ports without water,
our flesh cracked open, the bones laid bare, our souls dispersed,
almost completely destroyed.
Now the sea is undoing all that, the vast sea.

After boarding a little ship, we first traveled just to Jeju Island,
then we went to Japan in a bigger ship
but that's not real sea, just a little stream you can jump across.
Let's rather build a much larger ship, though it take three years.
We've come into possession of a vast sea, a wide sky.
Let's board a large ship and set out.

We will cleave the waves, force a way through storms,
pierce the horizon where it touches the sky.
Let's give a great cry and then set out.
Hearts trapped in ports without water,
let's rise up together. The sea is your home.
We are unfettered souls, a liberated people,

우리들 사슬 벗은 넋이로다 풀어 놓인 겨레로다
가슴엔 잔뜩 별을 안으려마
손에 잡히는 엄마 별 아가 별
머리엔 그득 보배를 이고 오렴
발 아래 좍 깔린 산호요 진주라
바다로 가자 우리 큰 바다로 가자

eagerly embracing a myriad stars;

in my hands are mother stars, baby stars.

Come with heads crowned in jewels.

Coral and pearls crunch beneath our feet.

Let's go down to the sea, let's all go down to the vast sea.

Note: Jeju Island is a part of Korea. It lies some way off the southwestern coast.

땅거미

가을날 땅거미 아렴풋한 흐름 위를
고요히 실리우다 휜뜻 스러지는 것
잊은 봄 보랏빛의 낡은 내음이뇨
이미 사라진 천리 밖의 산울림
오랜 세월 시닷긴 으스름한 파스텔

애닯은 듯한
좀 서러운 듯한

오! 모두 다 못 돌아오는
먼— 지난날의 놓친 마음

원래제목: 놓인 마음

Twilight

Is this the ancient smell of a forgotten springtime violet hue
that is being quietly swept over the dim flow
of an autumn twilight then gently vanishing in a flash?
My love's lost mountain echo a thousand *ri* away,
pastels long-ago washed, polished, faded dim.

Pitiful seeming,
sorrowful seeming.

Oh! All unable ever to return again,
the lost heart of far-away, long past days.

Original title: "Lost Heart."

새벽의 처형장

새벽의 처형장에는 서리 찬 마의 숨결이 획 획 살을 에웁니다
탕탕 탕탕탕 퍽퍽 쓰러집니다
모두가 씩씩한 맑은 눈을 가진 젊은이들
낳기 전에 임을 빼앗긴 태극기를 도루 찾아
3년을 휘두르며 바른 길을 앞서 걷던 젊은이들
탕탕탕 탕탕 자꾸 쓰러집니다
연유 모를 떼죽음 원통한 떼죽음
마지막 숨이 다져질 때에도 못 잊는 것은
하현 찬 달 아래 중고산(鐘鼓山) 머리 나르는 태극기
오— 망해 가는 조국의 모습
눈이 차마 감겨 졌을까요
보아요 저 흘러내리는 싸늘한 피의 줄기를
피를 흠뻑 마신 그 해가 일곱 번 다시 뜨도록
비린내는 죽음의 거리를 휩쓸고 숨 다졌나니
처형이 잠시 쉬는 그 새벽마다
피를 씻는 물차 눈물을 퍼부어도 퍼부어도
보아요 저 흘러내리는 생혈의 싸늘한 핏줄기를

Execution Yard at Dawn

In the execution yard at dawn an icy breath of evil pierces the flesh.

Bang, bang, thud. Each falls.

All fresh-eyed youths, who for the past three years had led the quest

for the right way ahead, waving the beloved Korean flag they had been robbed of

long before they were born, and had recovered three years before.

Bang, bang, thud. They keep falling.

Groundless mass deaths, appalling deaths.

One thing they cannot forget, to the very last breath,

the Korean flag flying high on Jonggosan under a cold white moon.

Oh—image of this nation as it heads for ruin.

How could they bear to close their eyes?

See, that trickle of icy blood flowing down.

While that sun that drank its fill of blood rises another seven times

they sweep and cover the streets of stinking death.

Each dawn, while executions cease for a while,

a water cart washes away the blood, though tears flow and flow.

See, that trickle of icy life-blood flowing down.

Note: This poem evokes a tragic incident in the post-independence conflict between leftists and right-wing groups in Yeosu, South Jeolla Province, in 1947. Jonggosan is a hill rising above Yeosu harbor.

절망

옥천(玉川) 긴 언덕에 쓰러진 죽음 떼죽음
생혈은 쏟고 흘러 십리 강물이 붉었나이다
싸늘한 가을바람 사흘 불어 피 강물은 얼었나이다
이 무슨 악착한 죽음이오니까
이 무슨 전세에 없던 참변이오니까
조국을 지켜 주리라 믿은 우리 군병의 창 끝에
태극기는 갈가리 찢기고 불타고 있습니다
별 같은 청춘의 그 충충한 눈들은
악의 독주(毒酒)에 가득 취한 군병의 칼 끝에
모조리 도려 빼이고 불타 죽었나이다
이 무슨 재변이오니까
우리의 피는 그리도 불순한 바 있었나이까
이 무슨 정치의 이름아래
무슨 뼈에 사무친 원수였기에
훗한 겨레의 아들딸이었을 뿐인데
이렇게 유황불에 타 죽고 말았나이까
근원이 무에든지 캘 바이 아닙니다
죽어도 죽어도 이렇게 죽는 수도 있나이까
산 채로 살을 깎이어 죽었나이다
산 채로 눈을 뽑혀 죽었나이다
칼로가 아니라 탄환으로 쏘아서 사지를 갈가리 끊어 불태웠나이다
훗한 겨레의 피에도 이러한 불순한 피가 섞여 있음을 이제 참으로 알았나이다
아! 내 불순한 핏줄 저주 받을 핏줄
산 고랑이나 개천가에 버려둔 채 까맣게 연독(鉛毒)한 죽음의 하나하나
탄환이 쉰 방 일흔 방 여든 방 구멍이 뚫고 나갔습니다

Despair

Fallen on long ridges, along pure streams, so many corpses,

life-blood gushing out, flowing, the riverside crimson for miles.

For three days a chill wind blew, the blood-red river froze.

What appalling corpses are these?

What horror is this, never known before?

Our soldiers believed they were defending the nation, but at the tip of their spears

the national flag is ferociously torn to shreds and burned.

The fast-flowing tears of those jade-like youths

were all scattered far and wide, burned to death

at the tip of the swords of those soldiers, utterly drunken with the hard liquor of evil.

What disaster is this?

Was there such an impure intention infecting our blood?

In the name of what policy

did they end up devoured in such a brimstone blaze,

seen as our enemies to the core

though they were really our docile people's sons and daughters?

No matter what the reason, it is not worth exploring.

Alive, their flesh was slashed, they died.

Alive, their eyes were put out, they died.

Their limbs were detached, not by swords but by bullets,

then they were burned. Now I realize:

impure blood has mingled with our docile people's blood.

Ah, my impure blood-stream, blood-stream fit to be cursed!

Corpses dumped one by one in mountain furrows or alongside streams, stiff and black.

Bullets pierced them, fifty, seventy, eighty each.

The younger brother killed his elder brother, yes, truly.

아우가 형을 죽였는데 이렇소이다
조카가 아재를 죽였는데 이렇소이다
무슨 뼈에 사무친 원수였기에
무슨 정치의 말을 썼기에
이래도 이 민족에 희망을 부쳐 볼 수 있사오리까
생각은 끊기고 눈물만 흐릅니다

The nephew killed his uncle, yes, truly.

If they were our enemies to the core,

using the words of what policy

can we still speak of hope to this nation?

I abandon thought and only weep.

Note: This poem too evokes the violent, fratricidal conflicts that tore Korea apart in the years following 1945.

겨레의 새해

해는 저물 적마다 그가 저지른 모든 일을 잊음의 큰 바다로 흘려보내지만
우리는 새해를 오직 보람으로 다시 맞이한다
멀리 사천이백팔십일 년
한뫼에 흰 눈이 쌓인 그대로
겨레는 한결같이 늘고 커지도다
일어나고 없어지고 온갖 살림은
구태여 캐내어 따질 것 없어
긴 긴 반만년 통틀어 오롯했다
사십 년 치욕은 한바탕 험한 꿈
사 년 쓰린 생각 아직도 눈물이 돼
이 아침 이 가슴 정말 뻐근하거니
나라가 처음 만방 평화의 큰 기둥 되고
백성이 인류 위해 큰일을 맡음이라
긴 반만년 합쳐서 한 해로다
새해 처음 맞는 겨레의 새해
미진한 대업 이루리라 거칠 것 없이 닫는 새해
이 첫날 겨레는 손 맞잡고 노래한다

The Nation's New Year

Every time the sun sets, it pours every spoiled thing into Oblivion's vast ocean.

We welcome the new year, full of promise.

Stretching into the distance, the year 4281,

with white snow piled on white mountains!

Our nation is constantly growing and expanding.

Rising up, then abolished, all its life

has been perfect, no need to check further,

throughout its lengthy five thousand years.

The forty years of shame are a scrap of stormy dream.

The burning thought of these past four years still brings tears.

This morning my heart is truly anguished.

The nation should become a pillar of far-reaching peace!

Our people are charged with great tasks for humanity.

One year, combining, combining with those five thousand years,

a new year for our people as they first greet the new year,

the new year arrives valiantly to fulfill an unfinished great task.

On this first day, the people are singing hand in hand.

연 2

좀평나무 높은 가지 끝에 얽힌 다아 해진 흰 실낱을 남은 몰라도
보름 전에 산을 넘어 멀리 가버린 내 연의 한 알 남긴 설움의 첫 씨
태어난 뒤 처음 높이 띄운 보람 맛본 보람
안 끊어졌드면 그럴 수 없지
찬바람 쐬며 콧물 흘리며 그 겨울내 그 실낱 치어다 보러 다녔으리
내 인생이란 그때부터 벌써 시든 상 싶어
철든 어른을 뽐내다가도 그 실낱 같은 병(病)의 실마리
마음 어느 한 구석에 도사리고 있어 얼씬거리면
아이고! 모르지
불다 자는 바람 타다 꺼진 불똥
아! 인생도 겨레도 다아 멀어지던구나

Kite 2

Other people were unaware of the scrap of frayed white thread tangled at the tip of a high branch of a nettle tree.

It was a first seed of sorrow, left by my kite as it went sailing away beyond the hills two weeks before,

the joy of a high-flying kite, the first of my life, and if it had not snapped

that would not have been the case.

I would have kept on playing, gazing up at that string all winter long, out in the cold wind, nose running.

I have the impression that my life began to wither from that moment on.

Though I vaunt my maturity, a hint of disease like that scrap of thread

has lurked in a corner of my heart, sometimes appearing

but then, alas! nobody knows.

Wind blows, then falls. A flickering spark expires.

Ah, a life, and the country too, all fade far away.

망각

걷던 걸음을 멈추고 서서도 얼컥 생각키는 것 죽음이로다
그 죽음이사 서른 살 쩍에 벌써 다 잊어버리고 살아왔는데
웬 노릇인지 요즘 자꾸 그 죽음 바로 닥쳐온 듯만 싶어져
항용 주춤 서서 행길을 호기로이 달리는 행상(行喪)을 보랐고 있느니

내 가버린 뒤도 세월이야 그대로 흐르고 흘러가면 그뿐이오라
나를 안아 기르던 산천도 만년 한양 그 모습 아름다워라
영영 가버린 날과 이 세상 아무 가겔 것 없으매
다시 찾고 부를 인들 있으랴 억만 영겁이 아득할 뿐

산천이 아름다워도 노래가 고왔더라도 사랑과 예술이 쓰고 달콤하여도
그저 허무한 노릇이어라 모든 산다는 것 다 허무하오라
짧은 그 동안이 행복했던들 참다웠던들 무어 얼마나 다를라더냐
다 마찬가지 아니 남만 나을러냐? 다 허무하오라

그날 빛나던 두 눈 딱 감기어 명상한대도 눈물은 흐르고 허덕이다 숨 다 지면 가는 거지야
더구나 총칼 사이 헤매다 죽는 태어난 비운의 겨레이어든
죽음이 무서웁다 새삼스레 뉘 비겁할소냐마는 비겁할소냐마는
죽는다 - 고만이라 - 이 허망한 생각 내 마음을 왜 꼭 붙잡고 놓질 않느냐
망각하자 - 해 본다 지난날을 아니라 닥쳐오는 내 죽음을
아! 죽음도 망각할 수 있는 것이라면

허나 어디 죽음이사 망각해 질 수 있는 것이냐
길고 먼 세기는 그 죽음 다 망각하였지만

Forgetfulness

As I stop walking and just stand here, the thought of death arises.
Death! I lived in forgetfulness of that when I was thirty,
but for some reason nowadays I keep feeling that death is approaching.
As I stand hesitating by a roadside, a funeral procession passes boldly.

After I am gone, time will keep on passing and passing, that's all.
The landscapes that embraced and nourished me
will remain beautiful for long ages to come.
The days that have gone forever have no relation with this world.

There is no one we can revisit or address; only, stretching before us, deserts of vast eternity.
Natural landscapes may be beautiful, songs lovely, love and art bitter-sweet,
still, all are vanity; all that life brings is vanity.
One brief moment may be happy or true, but what difference does that make?

It's all the same, being born or not—all vanity.
On that day, we close our once-bright eyes in meditation, tears flow, a few gasps, one last breath, then we are gone.
Because I was born in a tragic nation, wandering between guns and swords until death,
even if I say I fear death no one will call me cowardly, a coward.
Death, the end, the thought that all was vanity perversely occupied my mind, would not let go.
I want to try to forget—not bygone days but my approaching death.
Ah, if only we could forget about death!

But how can death ever be forgotten?
Though this long-lasting century has forgotten all about it.

낮의 소란 소리

거나한 낮의 소란 소리 풍겼는데
금시 퇴락하는 양
묵은 벽지의 내음 그윽하고
저쯤에사 걸려 있을 희멀끔한 달
한 자락 펴진 구름도 못 말아놓는 바람이어니
묵근히 옮겨 딛는 밤의 검은 발짓만
고되인 넋을 짓밟누나
아! 몇 날을 더 몇 날을
뛰어 본다리 날아 본다리
허잔한 풍경을 안고 고요히 선다

원래제목: 발짓

Day's Uproar

Just as the brave young day's uproar spread

then soon vanished,

the smell of old wallpaper is deep.

A white, clean moon will soon hang aloft.

The wind cannot so much as roll up a single spread-out cloud.

Only night's dark footsteps, moving softly, trample over weary souls.

Ah! After leaping, flying

over so many days, so many days,

I now stand quietly, embracing an empty landscape.

Original title: "Footsteps."

감격 8·15

연옥의 반세기 짓밟히어 지늘끼고도 다시 선뜻 불같이 일어서는 우리는 대한의 훗한 겨레
쇠사슬 즈르릉 풀리던 그날
어디 하나 이단 있어 행렬을 빠져나더뇨
삼천만은 낱낱이 가슴 맺힌 독립을 외쳤을 뿐

강토가 까다로운 경위도(經緯度)에 자리했음 울어야 하느냐?
고구려 신라 적은 어찌들 했던가 뒤져 보려마
성조(聖祖) 이룩하신 이 땅은 천하의 양지
삼천리가 적어서 한이라면 영란토(英蘭土)를 보려마
기적이 아니더면 뫼실 수 없던 민족의 통령
그 총혜 그 담덩이 이 나라는 반석 위에 선 민주 보루

벌써 왜놈과의 싸움도 지난 듯싶은데
4년 동안은 누구들 때문에 흘린 피더냐
만년 공화의 세계 헌장 발맞추는 대한민국
민주 헌법이 그르더냐 토지개혁을 안 한다더냐
도시 대서양헌장이 미흡터란 말이지
48 대 6인데 6이 더 옳단 말이지
철의 장막은 숨 막혀도 독재하니 좋았고
민주 개방이 명랑하여도 인권 평등이 싫더란 말이지

40년 동안의 불 달음에도 얼은 남은 겨레로다
4년쯤의 싸움이사 우리는 백 년도 불가살이
이젠 벌써 시비를 따질 때가 아니로다
쓰러진 동지의 죽음을 밟고 넘어서 오직 전진할 뿐
대의에 죽음 영원한 삶임을 삼천만 모두 다 마음커니
대의 대한 그 앞에 간사한 모략과 흉측한 암투가 있을 수 없다
보라 저 피로 싸일 실지 회복의 수만 깃발
들어라 백만 총준의 지축을 흔드는 저 맹서들

August 15, 1945, Source of Inspiration

Trampled and oppressed, through fifty years of purgatory, the ardent folk of Korea readily rose again like a flame.

On the day we shook off our fetters

no one dissented or refused to join the processions.

All thirty million acclaimed the longed-for independence.

No need for our country to lament being where it is, or examine how things were in the days of Goguryeo and Silla.

This land, founded by our sacred ancestors, is in the best place.

You think our country is small? Just look at England!

Without a miracle, we could never have had such a leader.

That wisdom, that courage! This democracy built on a rock.

Surely, the war with the Japanese was already over.

So whose fault was all the blood shed over the past four years?

Korea is following the world's democratic constitutions.

You think the democratic constitution is wrong? Are they not going to carry out land reform?

You say the Atlantic Charter was far from satisfactory?

The voting was forty-eight to six; how could the six be right?

You want dictatorship, despite the dreadful iron curtain?

You reject equal human rights, despite the joys of democracy?

Even after forty years of fire, our nation still retains its spirit.

Four years of fighting is nothing; we will live for a century.

Now is not the time to argue about right and wrong.

We only have to move forward, over our fallen comrades.

We all believe: dying for a just cause is eternal life.

In a righteous Korea, there can be no deceit or feuds.

Lift high banners, demand the return of lost territories!

Stained with blood, the vows of the million wise who shake the earth.

오월 아침

비 개인 오월 아침
혼란스런 꾀꼬리 소리
찬엄(燦嚴)한 햇살 퍼져 오릅니다

이슬비 새벽을 적시울 즈음
두견의 가슴 찢는 소리 피어린 흐느낌
한 그릇 옛날 향훈(香薰)이 어찌
이 맘 흥건 안 젖었으리오마는

이 아침 새 빛에 하늘대는 어린 속잎들 저리 부드러웁고
그 보금자리에 찌찌찌 소리 내는 잘새의 발목은 포실거리어
접힌 마음 구긴 생각 이제 다 어루만져졌나 보오
꾀꼬리는 다시 창공을 흔드오
자랑찬 새 하늘을 사치스레 만드오

사향(麝香) 냄새도 잊어버렸대서야
불혹이 자랑이 아니 되오
아침 꾀꼬리에 안 불리는 혼이야
새벽 두견이 못 잡는 마음이야
한낮이 정밀(靜謐)하단들 또 무얼 하오

저 꾀꼬리 무던히 소년인가 보오
새벽 두견이야 오랜 중년이고
내사 불혹을 자랑턴 사람

Morning in May

One morning in May after rain has cleared
the call of the oriole rings out in confusion,
dazzling sunshine rises and spreads.

The moment light drizzle soaked the dawn
the cuckoo's heartbreaking blood-tinged sobs,
a bowlful of ancient fragrance,
inevitably soaked my heart

but this morning the fresh shoots swaying in the newborn light are soft,
and in the nests the cheeping fledglings' feet lie snug,
so my wrinkled heart and crumpled thoughts all seem to have been soothed.
The oriole makes the blue sky vibrate again,
rendering luxuriant the proud new heavens.

If I forget the fragrance of musk,
there would be no pride in having reached forty.
If my soul remains unmoved by the morning oriole,
my heart untouched by the dawn cuckoo,
what pride would there be in noon's serenity?

That oriole still seems a quite young boy,
the dawn cuckoo has long been middle-aged,
and I once was proud to have turned forty.

행군

북으로 북으로
울고 간다 기러기

남방 대숲 밑을
뉘 후여 날켰느뇨

낄르르 낄르
차운 어슨 달밤

언 하늘 스미지 못 해
처량한 행군

낄르! 가냘프게 멀다
하늘은 목메인 소리도 낸다

A March

Northward, northward
they fly, calling, the geese.

Who sent you flying off from beneath the bamboo groves
of the south?

Calling, calling,
on cold hazy moonlit nights.

Mournful march,
unable to merge with the distant sky.

So fragile, so far,
the sky too utters a choking sob.

수풀 아래 작은 샘

수풀 아래 작은 샘
언제나 흰 구름 떠가는 높은 하늘만 내어다보는
수풀 속의 맑은 샘
넓은 하늘의 수만 별을 그대로 총총 가슴에 박은 작은 샘
두레박을 쏟아져 동이 가를 깨지는 찬란한 떼별의 흘는 소리
얽혀져 잠긴 구슬손결이
온 별나라 휘흔들어 버리어도 맑은 샘
해도 저물 녘 그대 종종걸음 흰듯 다녀갈 뿐
그 밤 또 그대 날과 샘과 셋이 도른도른
무슨 그리 향그런 이야기 날을 새웠나
샘은 애끈한 젊은 꿈 이제도 그저 지녔으리
이 밤 내 혼자 내려가 볼까나 내려가 볼까나

A Little Well Beneath a Bush

A little well beneath a bush,

ever only gazing up at the distant sky with its drifting clouds,

that pure well beneath a bush

keeping the vast sky's myriad stars imprinted dense within its breast, that little well,

the sound of those dazzling stars being poured from the bucket

and breaking against the edge of the water pot,

though jewel hands, tightly locked together,

shake that realm of stars, the well remains pure.

At sunset you quickly come and go, and though the well is lonesome,

that night again, you and I and the well, we three together,

spend the whole night exchanging fragrant words

but the well is still just cherishing its youthful dreams,

so this evening shall I go down there alone and look,

go down and look?

언 땅 한 길

언 땅 한 길 파도 파도
괭이는 아프게 마치더라
언 대로 묻어 두기 불쌍하기사
봄 되어 녹으면 울며 보채리

두 자 세 치를 눈이 덮여도
뿌리는 얼씬 못 건드려
대 죽고 난 이 3월 파르스름히
풀잎은 깔리네 깔리네

Digging in Frozen Ground

Digging deep in frozen ground, dig as one may
the pickaxe jars painfully.
It's a pity to leave it buried, frozen,
but it will melt when spring comes, then it will cry and whine.

Even covered with more than two feet of snow,
the roots won't be touched
and in the springtime months, though the stalks seemed dead,
green grass will spread and spread.

지반추억(池畔追憶)

깊은 겨울 햇빛이 다사한 날
큰 못가의 하마 잊었던 두둑 길을 사뿐 거닐어 가다 무심코 주저앉다
구을다 남어 한곳에 소복이 쌓인 낙엽 그 위에 주저앉다
살르 빠시식 어쩌면 내가 이리 짓궂은고
내 몸피를 내가 느끼거늘 아무렇지도 않은 듯 앉어지다?
못물은 추위에도 닳는다 얼지도 않는 날씨 낙엽이 수없이 묻힌 검은 펄
흙이랑 더러 드러나는 물 부피도 많이 줄었다
흐르질 않더라도 가는 물결이 금 지거늘
이 못물 왜 이럴꼬 이게 바로 그 죽음의 물일까
그저 고요하다 뻘 흙 속엔 지렁이 하나도 꿈틀거리지 않어?
뽀글하지도 않어 그저 고요하다 그 물 위에 떨어지는 마른 잎 하나도 없어?
햇볕이 다사롭기야 나는 서어하나마 인생을 느끼는데
여남은 해? 그때는 봄날이러라 바로 이 못가이러라
그이와 단둘이 흰모시 진솔 두르고 푸르른 이끼도 행여 밟을세라 돌 위에 앉고
부풀은 봄 물결 위의 떠 노는 백조를 희롱하여
아직 청춘을 서로 좋아하였었거니
아! 나는 이즈음 서어하나마 이생(人生)을 느끼는데

Memories of a Pondside Stroll

One midwinter's day with warm sunshine,

after walking light-footed along a nearly forgotten hill-path at the side of a large pond

I chance to sit down. At one place dead leaves have rolled together in a heap and there I sit.

Rustle, crunch, I seem to be disturbing them.

Is it right to sit down so thoughtlessly when I can feel my frame?

Despite the cold, the pond is warm, the weather not freezing,

and with the black mud of the edge where countless leaves are buried the volume of water visible is much reduced.

Though it is not flowing, slight ripples run and I wonder what has happened to this pondwater;

might these be the waters of death?

Utterly quiet, and in the mud along the edge is there not a single worm squirming?

Not one wriggling? Utterly quiet. Is there not a single dry leaf falling onto the water?

Since the sunlight is warm I feel alive, though not enough.

Some ten years ago, was it? It must have been springtime, by this very pond.

We both were wearing new cloths of white ramie, sitting on a rock, anxious not to crush green moss,

we mocked the swans afloat on the swollen spring waves.

Each of us enjoyed the spring of our youth

and now, ah, I feel alive despite regrets.

천리를 올라온다

천리를 올라온다
또 천리를 올라들 온다
나귀 얼렁 소리 닿는 말굽 소리
청운의 큰 뜻은 모여들다 모여들다

남산 북악 갈래갈래 뻗은 골짜기
엷은 안개 그 밑에 묵은 이끼와 푸른 송백
낭낭히 울려 나는 청의동자(靑衣童子)의 글 외는 소리
나라가 덩그러히 이룩해 지다

인정이 울어 팔문(八門)이 굳이 닫치어도
난신 외구(亂臣外寇) 더러 성을 넘고 불을 놓다
퇴락한 금석 전각(金石殿閣) 이젠 차라리 겨레의 향그런 재화로다
찬란한 파고다여 우리 그대 앞에 진정 고개 숙인다

철마가 터지던 날 노들 무쇠다리
신기한 먼 나라를 사뿐 옮겨다 놓았다
서울! 이 나라의 화사한 아침 저자러라
겨레의 새 봄바람에 어리둥절 실행(失行)한 숫처녀들 없었을 거냐

남산에 올라 북한 관악을 두루 바라다보아도
정녕코 산정기로 태어난 우리들이라
우뚝 솟은 멧부리마다 고물고물 골짜기마다
내 모습 내 마음 두견이 울고 두견이 피고

Coming from Far Away

Some are coming from far far away.
Others, too, are coming from far far away.
Donkeys clattering, horses cantering,
full of lofty dreams they are gathering, gathering.

In the valleys that crisscross Namsan and Bukhansan
where ancient moss and green pines flourish amidst light mist
boyish voices ring brightly as they recite their lessons.
Our nation is being firmly reestablished.

Though the city's eight gates were shut tight at curfew,
traitors, raiders crossed the walls, set fire to the town.
The royal palaces' stones, dilapidated now,
testify clearly to our people's great refinement of talent.

Glorious Pagoda Park! We bow in veneration before you.
The day the railway came, the bridge across the Han,
it brought us mysterious, distant lands.
Seoul! Our nation's luxurious morning market!

Surely there must have been young girls who misbehaved
quite confounded at our country's new spring breeze!
If you climb Namsan, gaze at Bukhansan, Gwanaksan,
it is quite clear we are a people born of mountain forces.

높은 재 얕은 골 흔들리는 실마리 길
그윽하고 너그럽고 잔잔하고 산뜻하지
백마 호통소리 나는 날이면
황금 꾀꼬리 희비(喜悲) 교향(交響)을 아뢰니라

On each soaring peak, in each meandering valley,

my face, my heart, cuckoos singing, azaleas blooming.

Lofty peaks, deep valleys, narrow winding paths, so sweet, so generous, so peaceful and bright!

On the day when men on white horses cry aloud their summons,

golden orioles will respond in symphonies of joy and sorrow.

Note: Namsan and Bukhansan are the hills enclosing the original city of Seoul to south and north; Gwanaksan lies to the south across the Han River, visible from Namsan though quite far away. Pagoda Park, now called Tapgol Park, in central Seoul, was the place where on March 1, 1919, the Independence Movement was launched.

어느 날 어느 때고

어느 날 어느 때고
잘 가기 위하여
평안히 가기 위하여

몸이 비록
아프고 지칠지라도
마음 평안히
가기 위하여

일만 정성
모두어 보리

덧없이 봄은 살같이 떠나고
중년은 하 외로워도
이 허무에선 떠나야 될 것을

살이 삭삭
여미고 썰릴지라도
마음 평안히
가기 위하여

아! 이것
평생을 닦는 좁은 길

Every Day, at Every Time

Every day, at every time,
in order to depart well,
in order to depart peacefully,

even if the body
is sick and weary,
in order for the heart
to depart peacefully,

I will undertake every task
with entire sincerity.

Spring is gone in a flash, like an arrow,
and though my middle years may be very lonesome
I must cast off this sense of emptiness.

Yet my flesh
is snipped and chopped away,
in order for the heart
to depart peacefully.

Ah! That's
a narrow path that needs to be sought for one whole lifetime.

오월 한

모란이 피는 오월 달
월계도 피는 오월 달
온갖 재앙이 다 벌어졌어도
내 품에 남는 다순 김 있어
마음 실 튀기는 오월이러라

무슨 대견한 옛날였으랴
그래서 못 잊는 오월이랴
청산을 거닐면 하루 한 치씩
뻗어 오르는 풀숲 사이를
보람만 달리는 오월이러라

아무리 두견이 애닯아 해도
황금 꾀꼬리 아양을 펴도
싫고 좋고 그렇기보다는
풍기는 내음에 지늘꼈건만
어느새 다 해진 오월(五月)이러라

Maytime Regrets

Month of May when peonies bloom,
month of May when laurels bloom, too.
No matter all the misfortunes I undergo,
in my heart there remains a warm path
and my heart-strings ring in the month of May.

It's not because of memorable bygone days.
I can never forget May.
In May, as I walk over the hills,
recompense comes hastening swift
amidst bushes that grow an inch each day.

In May, though the cuckoo may sing, heartbroken,
and the golden warbler woo,
I do not feel dislike or liking.
Instead I am captivated by the fragrance.
May is over in a flash

Memories of My Father

Harold Kim Hyeon-cheol

When I recall my father, the first images that come to mind are things like his heavy build and sonorous voice; his white ramie clothes; his black coat; his intense enthusiasm for Western classical music and Korean traditional music; his performances on Korean instruments such as the gayageum, the gomeungo, the drum, the zither; his fondness for liquor, for anti-Japanese activities, for democracy. As for food he disliked anything made of wheat flour, and he never ate rice-cake. It is nearly sixty years since Father died; my memories have grown dim, and I have forgotten many things, but I will try to write down what I can remember.

When others saw him, his sturdy bearing and his sonorous, clear voice encouraged them to take him for a hearty, robust kind of person, but actually, deep inside, he was very different—extremely sensitive and strongly emotional. If he experienced sorrow, he felt it far more intensely than most people; whenever he discovered beauty, he tended to be much more intensely fascinated by it than most others.

There are many examples I might give but you will best understand if I refer to some familiar stories. When he was studying in Japan, he obtained a postcard with a photo of the famous French beauty Mignon, and he is reputed to have wept frequently at the sight of her innocent, touching beauty. The fact that the sight of a beautiful face made him weep . . . If he had been like other people, at most he might have gone as far as to give a faint sigh at the sight of such touching beauty, but I think there are very few people who would weep as he did. Toward the end of his infatuation with Mignon, he wrote a poem on the back of her photo. Let me quote the opening lines:

> On moonlit nights, and dew-filled mornings
> how many time did I embrace my Mignon and weep?
> [Study at] Aoyama sickened me in my youth,
> or rather it scattered the fragrance.
> A time for reciting poetry, a time for being poetic,
> a time for matching tears with tears,
> in those days my youth was already diseased
> but the bowl of fragrance never grew old . . .

Likewise, if you open the cover of his first volume of poems, published in 1935, you find on the title-page the words "A thing of beauty is a joy for ever" printed in English, a quotation from a poem by Keats. I assume that this indicates that he was a member of the aesthetic school of poets. Tender-hearted as he was, however, he was extremely strict toward his own children.

When I was in primary school, I used to long to join my friends from the nearby houses. Several times, seeing him sitting in a bamboo chair on the spacious porch of his quarters at home, his eyes tightly shut as if in prayer, immersed in poetic thoughts, I would bend low in the hope that Father would not open his eyes as I went speeding like an arrow loosed from the bow from the main house past the men's quarters in an attempted escape, but within half a second the call "Hyeon-cheol-a-a!" would ring out loudly in his sonorous voice, and I never once managed to escape successfully. Since I knew full well that a punishment awaited me if I did not go back into the house as soon as I was called, I had no choice but to obey.

He always used to say that I might get involved with bad kids if I played outside, so if there were friends I liked, I should phone them and invite them to come and play at our house. In the Gangjin of sixty years ago there were in all some one hundred telephones; our phone had the number 34. As a result, our home is full of beautiful memories of local children coming and playing merrily. When it was time for playing hide-and-seek in springtime, in the two long fields, each 20 yards by 5-6 yards, there were about a hundred peony bushes growing, and if any of us went and hid among them, he might find himself in real trouble.

When Father came home in a drunken state, all his children had to be standing in front of the gate to greet him; if one was missing, even because he had gone to the toilet, father would refuse to go inside until he appeared, but keep looking for him; as a result, an evening outing was something none of us could ever imagine. If any of us children came home after the sun had set and it had grown dark, without exception even the older brothers or sisters attending high school would be punished.

I remember once, when I was in the fourth grade of primary school, I called in at a friend's house on my way home from school and there, for the first time in my life, I saw a pack of flower-pattern playing cards lying on a desk; finding the pictures on them very pretty, I remarked to my friend, "What are these? They're pretty," and he replied, "That's a pack of flower-pattern cards; you can have them if you like." So I took them home and put them on the desk. Father saw them as he passed and became very angry; as soon as he knew where they had come from, he hurled them into the blazing fire in the kitchen hearth and, scolded me: "You are never again to touch such things." As a result, even now, some sixty years later, I have spent a whole lifetime as an idiot who has no idea how to play cards.

Father was so strict that I have no memory of him ever embracing any of us children. So when one day, much later, as I looked through the photograph album, I came across a picture of Father hugging me, I was amazed. At the thought that at least once he had held me, my heart brimmed over. One day, Mother tripped over a stone in the front yard and fell down. She had just noticed our grandfather approaching far in the distance. Father, who had been indoors, came hurrying out into the yard. I expected him to help mother up. But he just stood in front of her, looking down abstractedly and asking, "What's the matter? Are you all right?" I found it very odd that he did not take her hand and help her up. Later I asked my mother and learned that it was because Confucianism taught that if an older person was present, a father ought never to hold the hand or make any sign of affection toward wife or children. I suppose that nowadays, if husbands acted like that they would soon end up divorced.

Father had hoped to study vocal music at Tokyo Music College, but after hearing our grandfather stubbornly insist that, "Our eldest son cannot become an entertainer. If you intend to study singing, I shall be unable to pay your tuition," he gave up the idea of becoming a singer and used to say that his passion for music was consumed by literature instead. His dream of being a singer may not have been fulfilled, yet Father lived his whole life immersed in music. In those days, ebonite gramophone records each lasted just 3 minutes. With the Western classical music and the traditional Korean music contained on such records, listening to music became a daily routine for him, while his performance skills on traditional Korean instruments such as the geomungo, the gayageum, and the drum outshone those of professional players.

Singers of traditional Korean music such as Kim So-Hui, Bak Gwi-Hui, or Bak Cho-Weol, who later were to become famous nationwide, used to come to our house at Father's invitation to perform; they would come alone, without bringing a drummer to accompany them, and perform, with Father keeping time for them on the drum, since his skill was at least equal to any professional player's. Likewise, after he performed on the geomungo or gayageum they would be unstinting in their praise of his skill.

From the time I was about four until I started primary school, Father used to set me on his knee as he listened to Western classical music by the likes of Brahms, Beethoven, and Mozart, or Korean traditional music, instrumental or vocal, *pansori* or other forms of singing, and although in those times I used to fret at not being able to escape from the arms of a father who was fearsome as a tiger, looking back I realize that that was when I learned to appreciate and enjoy classical Western and Korean music. Since each side of a record only lasted three minutes or so, one whole symphony, especially Beethoven's ninth, required a set of up to ten records. As a result, one whole wall of the room was taken up with a mountainous pile of record albums.

The world-famous Rusian baritone Chaliapin or the violinist Mischa Elman performing in Seoul was a must; when a world-famous symphony orchestra came to Tokyo, or the world's top tenor Enrico Caruso performed there, Father would sell off fields, take the boat from Busan via Shimonoseki, and head for Tokyo. Of course, in those days there was no thought of such things as airplanes. Many scholars have written that Father's poetry was bound to have a special musical quality, since he was such a fanatic where music was concerned.

When Father was sixteen, he spent six months in Daegu prison for having been active in the Independence Movement. To celebrate his release, he purchased an English-Japanese dictionary. At that time there was no English-Korean dictionary. On the inside cover he wrote the words "commemorating my release from Daegu jail" and the date. Unfortunately, all his books as well as all our furniture disappeared during the Korean War, a great loss.

Prior to Liberation in 1945, we children were in constant trouble with our teachers at school on account of Father. My older sister and eldest brother were studying in Gwangju and

Seoul, and each of them was the only student in their class to refuse to adopt a Japanese name, keeping their Korean name. In their boarding houses, as vacation time approached, their teachers would summon them and threaten: "Tell your father that if you don't take Japanese names, you won't be allowed back in school." Completely unable to understand why they could not take Japanese names, the children would weep as they repeated to Father that they would not be able to continue in school if they did not comply. But he replied casually, "All right, say you'll change names soon." Inevitably, they felt resentful.

Every Saturday, without fail, a Japanese policeman from the Gangjin police station would come and stamp the card left in a little box beside the gate leading to the men's quarters, certifying that Father was at home. In that way, the Japanese police checked that he had not left home to join the ranks of the Independence Movement. After stamping the card, the policeman would come in and admonish Father: "Tomorrow is Sunday, the day when every Japanese citizen pays a weekly visit to offer worship at the Shinto shrine; you must attend." But every week Father would give the same answer: "I have a chronic stomach ailment that obliges me to keep going to the toilet; if I have to go while I am at that sacred shrine, you'll send me to prison again, for sure." and the policeman would smile bitterly as he left, as if knowing that he would always get the same reply. Father also rejected the Japanese government's regulations requiring every Japanese citizen to have short hair, as can be clearly seen by his long hair in the photo taken at our grandfather's sixtieth birthday celebration, shortly before Liberation. Until Liberation, Father refused to perform Shinto worship, take a Japanese name, or cut his hair, and certainly he was not going to receive Japan's permission to work, while he himself did not wish for a job where he would be obliged to salute the Japanese flag at the start of work each day. As a result, inevitably, during the thirty-six years of Japanese rule our family's wealth slowly melted away.

When Father heard on the radio the news of Japan's defeat and the Liberation of our country that he had so longed to see, he could not hide his joy; he pulled out the Korean flag he had kept hidden deep in the chest of drawers inside a closet in his quarters, then the family with a few neighbors, following Father's directions, used crayons to quickly make a few hundred copies on sheets of white paper, which were then distributed among the people of Gangjin as they celebrated Liberation.

If there is one aspect of Father that I can never forget, it was his love of drink. His friends in those days used to say, exaggerating his capacity, "Yeongnang may not be able to carry four gallons of liquor on his back, he can carry them about in his belly." One day he came home just before nightfall, very drunk, dancing as he always did with both arms raised, while singing in a resonant voice the "Song of the Toreadors" from Bizet's opera "Carmen" in the original language. He would say something to Mother, who had gone into the kitchen for something, and when there was no reply, roared out, "Where have you got to?" and kick the pottery chamber pot that stood on the wood-floored porch. In those days, sixty years ago, everyone used these pots placed on the porch by night, rather than go all the way to the distant privy in the dark.

Everyone expected the pot to break as it fell into the yard but it must have been thick, it remained intact and we used it for many more years, until we moved up to Seoul. Father had been a football player in his school days, and in Gangjin he was the top player of softball tennis. I suppose it was called that because the ball used was much softer than the one used nowadays. Whenever he had free time, Father used to enjoy playing tennis with a few friends.

One day, I was puzzled to see a white-haired old man performing a deep bow before my father, who was sitting on the porch, but since I could not ask my tiger-fierce father, I went into the main house to ask Mother what the reason was. She explained that the old man had worked a piece of land belonging to Father for the past twenty years, and now Father had just given him the document transferring ownership of the land to him, and he was expressing his thanks in that way. The same thing happened several times after that. Father used to give bits of his land to those who had worked it for more than twenty years.

Once Liberation came, Father hoped to be given a role in the national reconstruction and stood as a candidate for the first Constitutional Assembly, but because he was poor at public relations, he lost. The successful candidate had mobilized his son, who was then attending a university in Seoul, and his friends, sending them all over Gangjin to campaign, while Father, insensitive to public opinion, took to riding a deluxe, private motor car that members of our family had sent down from Seoul as he went campaigning across the county, although it was most unlikely that the poor famers who made up the majority of the electorate would vote for anyone who not only belonged to the landowning class but also rode around in a deluxe automobile!

Until then Father had expressed his sorrow for the lost nation through his poems, but after Liberation he poured that passion into patriotic undertakings. In addition to being the local head of the then right-wing-leaning Korean Young Men's Association, Father was very active in groups such as the Korean Independence Promotion Assembly, which was the origin of many social groups working for the new Korean government. As a result, Father, active in such right-wing groups, become the target for the terrorist attacks that emanated from the South Korean Communist Party in those days.

One day in the spring of 1948, some of the members of the youth association who were guarding Father discovered materials that seemed destined to be used to burn the house down, hidden in two places, behind the tennis court and among the bamboos behind the main house. The police were called, and they confirmed that interpretation. Father found himself in a situation where the house was in danger of being burned down, and he had to consider the personal safety of himself and our family. In those days many leftists were being arrested by the police and enduring great hardships, while leading rightists fell victim to terrorist attacks from the left; it was a time of looming national tragedy.

Another factor underlying the move of our whole family to Seoul was the question of the children's education. Father, who had never once held any kind of paid employment, was already having difficulties paying the boarding charges of the two older children, who were studying in Seoul, and now, to make things even worse, I had been accepted to the same school, which meant yet more expense. So, two months before I was due to enter middle school, Father decided we should all move to Seoul. In the summer of 1948, he sold the house in Gangjin that he had so loved, and we moved to a house in the Sindang-dong neighborhood in eastern Seoul.

Once he had moved to Seoul, Father was very active in literary and cultural organizations, meeting almost every day with such noted figures as the poets Kim Gwang-seop, Bak Mok-weol, Seo Jeong-ju, or the critic Yi Heon-gu. Increasingly, they came to visit Father in our home. Some of them were people who were under severe popular censure for their pro-Japanese activities during the colonial period prior to 1945. One day, my older brother asked him, "That person is known to have been a pro-Japanese writer, is it okay for you to have relations with him?" Father nodded and replied, "I know what you mean. But in those days a lot of people who did not collaborate had nothing to eat. If we exclude people like that now, how many anti-Japanese writers will you be left with? In order not to encourage an even more virulent pro-Japanese clique, for the sake of our country we need to reach out to many such writers and give them the chance to collaborate in the construction of a new nation." My brother, dissatisfied with Father's reply, left the room with a sullen look. As a matter of fact, however, it would have been possible to count on one's fingers the writers who had never collaborated, so few they were, and looking back I believe that Father was right.

At the time, President Syngman Rhee's press secretary was the poet Kim Gwang-seop, Father's close friend. Urging Father to enter government service and help build the new nation, he offered him the choice between two possible jobs, as either vice-chief in the Bureau of Public Information or as director of the Publishing Bureau. After realizing that another close friend, the critic Yi Heon-gu, was intent on the position in the Bureau of Public Information, Father allowed him to take that position then accepted the job in the Publishing Bureau. Father's attitude in those days was that he would be satisfied with any kind of position allowing him to contribute to the good of the nation. However, although Father was determined to work wholeheartedly, the head of the Bureau of Public Information kept interfering in the work of the Publishing Bureau, and Father, who had never been subject to interference from anyone all his life, and unable to get along with his superior, quit the position after just seven months.

I recall a few incidents from that period. When I was in the third year of middle school, my school being close to the Central Government Building, I used to visit Father's office there almost every day on my way home, and if that coincided with the time Father was leaving work, I used to drive home with him in his car. What struck me in those days about Father's dress was the fact that he was virtually the only person working there to be wearing, as he always did, the traditional Korean long turumagi topcoat.

The picnic celebrating his appointment was held at Ttukseom Ferry, which is now well within Seoul city but in those days was a stretch of completely natural landscape, a level plain and a sandy beach beside the river with not a house in sight. While the employees were enjoying themselves swimming and playing various games, the twenty or so higher-level officials sitting around Father asked him to sing something. I had previously sometimes heard him sing a line or two after drinking a lot, but I had never heard him sing formally, so I was full of curiosity as I waited for him to start singing.

I suppose that most of the civil servants present were expecting one of the fashionable songs or ballads, but unexpectedly, from Father's lips emerged the unfamiliar tones of a traditional Korean poem, a *sijo*, sung on long-drawn-out notes. In a strong, resonant voice, he began to intone the ancient poem, "Blue stream flowing amidst green hills . . ." and immediately the faces of his audience changed into expressions of surprise and disappointment. It was only four years after Liberation, and they had grown up to the sound of Japanese pop-songs; they had probably never so much as heard a *sijo* being recited, and could not understand it. Seeing the situation from Father's viewpoint, in those days he had never had a chance to experience popular songs; he knew nothing except classical Western or Korean traditional music. He surely had no other option but to perform a *sijo*, transmitted as part of the traditional scholars' culture. In modern terms, their cultural norms did not correspond.

In April 1950, just two months before the outbreak of the war, the scriptwriter Seokyeong An Seok-ju died while still young. At the burial-ground, once the grave had been filled and covered, about ten writers sat down in a circle round the grave and drained a glass of soju each. In the midst of stories about their memories of the dead man, someone suddenly asked, "Hey, after Seokyeong, whose turn will it be to quit this world next?" and the gathering fell silent for a while.

I have been told that after a time, Father broke the silence by saying with a serious expression, "It will be my turn next." Since he looked well and had no health problems, the whole assembly refused to believe him and treated it as a joke. Yet only a little over five months later, on September 29, as he had prophesied, Father followed in An's footsteps and quit this life, to the great surprise of those who had been present that day.

At the start of the war on June 25, 1950, there had been a firm understanding that one of Father's best friends would meet us at the house with his automobile at 2 pm on June 27, and we would all head south together. But for some reason he did not appear as agreed, and it was late in the evening when Father learned by telephone that he had gone south alone. He was deeply disappointed by his friend's betrayal. At once, late though it was, he changed into farmer's clothing, with a barley-straw hat pressed low over his face, left our home and went to our relative's house. The North Korean army entered Seoul in the morning of June 28, only about ten hours later.

North Korean soldiers stationed guards in front of the gate of our house in Sindang-dong, on duty day and night, intending ultimately to force Father and our whole family to go north, and in the meantime observing our comings and goings. Actually, knowing that Father had gone into hiding just before the North Korean army entered Seoul, presumably they were waiting to see if perhaps he might visit the house secretly by night. The rest of us spent the days quietly waiting, hoping that one day the guards might leave the house unguarded briefly while they had lunch or supper, having completed all our preparations for flight. Finally, the guards briefly left the house unguarded one day at lunchtime; we all managed to escape and were reunited with Father in the house of a relative where he was hiding.

During the three months of North Korean rule, we stayed hidden in our relative's house. When the North Korean retreat came on September 28, shells rained down on the city's residential areas, causing many victims. Father had been hiding in the house's air-raid shelter but seeing how more and more women from the neighborhood were coming to shelter there, since it was very small he went out to make room for them, only to be struck a mortal wound by shrapnel from a shell fired by the retreating North Koreans, and he fell, never to recover.

Deeply shocked and saddened by the loss of Father, the rest of us wearily went back to the Sindang-dong house we had escaped from three months earlier. On January 4, 1951, the North Korean army and the Chinese Army reinvaded Seoul. Our family fled south for refuge and only came back in December 1951. All that remained of our house were the front gate and the walls. Window-frames and the porch's wooden floor were gone, ripped up and carted off, while not a single volume of books remained, or any furnishings; all had been plundered. That meant that we were left without a single relic or keepsake. In later years, we were so poor that we could not usually afford the fare to come to Gangjin when events were organized in memory of Father. Then I left for the United States and for many years did not visit Korea at all . . .

Finally, in 2008, Father was posthumously awarded the Korean government's highest recognition for achievement in the field of culture, the Gold Crown Order of Cultural Merit. On October 18 that year, I was honored to receive the award from the hands of the Minister of Culture, Tourism and Sport on behalf of the President of the Republic of Korea. That, together with the annual Yeong-Nang Festival organized nowadays at Gangjin, gives me the assurance that, despite the passage of time, he is far from being forgotten.

Poem Titles

끝없는 강물이 흐르네 2
An Endless River Flows 3
어덕에 바로 누워 4
As I Lay Stretched Out on a Hill 5
"오-매 단풍 들겄네" 6
"Why, Autumn Colors Are Coming!" 7
제야(除夜) 8
New Year's Eve 9
쓸쓸한 뫼 앞에 10
Before a Desolate Grave 11
함박눈 12
Falling Snowflakes 13
돌담에 속삭이는 햇발 14
Sunlight Whispering on Stone Walls 15
꿈 밭에 봄마음 16
A Springtime Heart Off to Fields in Dreams 17
가늘한 내음 18
Faint Perfume 19
내 옛날 온 꿈이 20
Dreams I Used to Have 21
내 마음을 아실 이 22
Someone Who Knows My Heart 23

시냇물 소리 24
The Sound of a Stream 25
뉘 눈결에 쏘이었소 26
Stung by a Look 27
눈물에 실려 가면 28
Borne on Tears 29
그대는 호령도 하실 만하다 30
You Are Worthy to Speak in a Commanding Tone 31
아파 누워 32
Lying Sick Alone, I Pray 33
물 보면 흐르고 34
At the Sight of Water 35
강선대(降仙臺) 돌바늘 끝에 36
At the Tip of the Gangseondae Rock Pinacle 37
사개 틀린 고풍(古風)의 툇마루에 38
On an Old-style Twisted Dovetail Back-porch 39
불지암(佛地庵) 40
Bulji-am, Buddha-World Hermitage 41
모란이 피기까지는 42
Until Peonies Bloom 43
두견(杜鵑) 44
The Cuckoo 45

청명 (淸明) 48
Brightness 49
황홀한 달빛 52
Intoxicating Moonlight 53
마당 앞 맑은 새암을 54
The Clear Well in Front of the Yard 55
뵈지도 않는 입김 58
님 두시고 가는 길의 58
무너진 성터에 58
저녁때 저녁때 58
Unseen Breath 59
Setting Off After Leaving My Love 59
Over Ruined City Walls 59
At Evening, at Evening 59
풀 위에 맺어지는 60
푸른 향물 흘러 버린 60
좁은 길가에 60
허리띠 매는 새악시 60
Pearling over Grass 61
Blue Fragrance Has Faded 61
Beside a Narrow Path 61
A Girl Tying Her Sash 61
못 오실 임이 그리웁기로 62
다정히도 불어오는 62
향내 없다고 버리시려면 62
어덕에 누워 62
Longing for My Lover Who Cannot Come 63
Blowing Affectionately 63

Discarded for Having No Fragrance 63
When I Lie on a Hill 63
밤사람 그립고야 64
눈물 속 빛나는 보람과 64
빈 포케트에 64
바람에 나부끼는 깔잎 64
I Yearn for a Nighttime Companion! 65
The Bright Recompense in Tears 65
I Thrust My Hand into an Empty Pocket 65
Reeds Trembling in the Breeze 65
뻘은 가슴을 66
그 밖에 더 아실 이 66
밤이면 고총 아래 66
저 곡조만 66
Mudflats Brightly Bare Their Breasts 67
How Could Anyone Else Know 67
In the Lee of an Old Grave by Night 67
If Its Melody 67
산골을 놀이터로 68
사랑은 깊으기 68
빠른 철로에 68
숲 향기 숨길을 68
A Valley for Her Playground 69
Love Is as Deep 69
On an Express Train 69
The Forest's Fragrance Took My Breath Away 69
그 색시 서럽다 70
떠 날아가는 마음의 70

미움이란 말 속에 70
생각하면 부끄러운 70
온몸을 감도는 70
That Girl Is Sorrowful 71
My Drifting Mind 71
Within the Word Hatred 71
I Feel Ashamed When I Remember the Days 71
Circling My Body 71
거문고 74
A Geomungo 75
가야금 76
A Gayageum 77
빛깔 환히 78
A Ray of Light Brightly 79
연 1 80
Kite 1 81
오 월 82
May 83
독을 차고 84
Carrying Poison 85
묘비명 86
Memorial 87
한줌 흙 88
A Handful of Dust 89
강물 90
A River 91
한길에 누워 92
Lying in the Middle of the Road 93

우감 (偶感) 94
A Sudden Feeling 95
내 훗진 노래 96
My Solitary Song 97
춘향 98
Chunhyang 99
집 104
A House 105
북 108
Drum 109
바다로 가자 110
Let's Go Down to the Sea 111
땅거미 114
Twilight 115
새벽의 처형장 116
Execution Yard at Dawn 117
절망 118
Despair 119
겨레의 새해 122
The Nation's New Year 123
연 2 124
Kite 2 125
망각 126
Forgetfulness 127
낮의 소란 소리 128
Day's Uproar 129
감격 8.15 130
August 15, 1945, Source of Inspiration 131

오월 아침 132

Morning in May 133

행군 134

A March 135

수풀 아래 작은 샘 136

A Little Well Beneath a Bush 137

언 땅 한 길 138

Digging in Frozen Ground 139

지반추억(池畔追憶) 140

Memories of a Pondside Stroll 141

천리를 올라온다 142

Coming from Far Away 143

어느 날 어느 때고 146

Every Day, at Every Time 147

오월 한 148

Maytime Regrets 149